Just in Time

IMMEDIATE HELP FOR
THE TIME PRESSURED

Just In Time

IMMEDIATE HELP FOR
THE TIME-PRESSURED

Robert D. Rutherford, Ph.D.

KENERIC PUBLISHING CO.
Boulder, Colorado

Originally published by John Wiley & Sons, Inc. Copyright 1981 by Robert D. Rutherford.

Keneric Publishing Company Edition 1984.
  First printing March, 1984
  Second printing August, 1984
  Third printing January, 1988
  Fourth printing July, 1988

This publication is designed to provide accurate and authoritative information in regard to the subject matter covered. It is sold with the understanding that the publisher is not engaged in rendering legal, accounting, or other professional service. If legal advice or other expert assistance is required, the services of a competent professional person should be sought. *From a Declaration of Principles jointly adopted by a Committee of the American Bar Association and a Committee of Publishers.*

Library of Congress Cataloging in Publication Data:
Rutherford, Robert D.
  Just in Time.

  Includes index.
  1. Time management. I. Title.

HD38.R85   658.4'093   80-22409
ISBN 0-932590-02-0 (casebound)

Printed in the United States of America
10 9 8 7 6 5 4 3 2 1

Preface

Just In Time deals with the time questions most frequently asked of managers, executives, and professionals—questions that have emerged over and over among the several thousands who have participated in my time management workshops across the United States, Canada, and Mexico. This book provides easy access to these questions and responses, and it is designed so that the busy professional can turn immediately to the particular time problem or pressure he or she is experiencing. Each question is self-contained. Each response is written directly to you, the reader, with the intention of striking at the core of the time problem.

The questions are grouped into eight chapters, which describe general categories of time management, and the table of contents lists all seventy questions included under these eight general headings. Browse through the table of contents to get a feel for the general organization of the book. The questions themselves may help you to identify time problems that you face and perhaps are not conscious of.

Once you are familiar with the table of contents it is a simple matter to glance through it and pinpoint the particular problem you need help with. Are you having trouble delegating? Scan the questions listed under "Delegation—The Key to Managerial Sanity" to find the one appropriate to your needs. It is not necessary to read the book from cover to cover.

Use the book as a ready reference, as a source book to be picked up and read when you face a particular time pressure. Let the responses help you to determine what is really happening to your time and to remind you how you can deal with your time challenges more powerfully.

ROBERT D. RUTHERFORD

Boulder, Colorado
December 1980

Acknowledgments

Just in Time was written in direct response to questions asked by many of the thousands of individuals who have participated in the national Time Effectiveness workshops I conduct regularly in the United States, Canada, and Mexico. It was written because I saw a need—the need for a book that would focus on what really happens with time and that would place the responsibility and accountability for managing time where it belongs.

I have been privileged to work with people from all walks of life—people who were concerned about their time and who expressed a serious desire to get more out of their work and life. It is to all these individuals that this book is dedicated.

Special acknowledgments for help in putting *Just in Time* together go to Barbara Rice, for her valuable suggestions in organizing the text, for her contribution to the Time Effectiveness workshops, and for being a friend, colleague, and sounding board for many of the ideas expressed in the book; to Mary Hey, who worked closely with me on the drafting and editing of the manuscript, who caringly challenged my writing style, who encouraged greater clarity, and who made many valuable suggestions throughout the work; to Beth Haas, for typing the manuscript and for suggestions and help in getting the material ready for publication; to Rick Nachman of Management Research Corp., for his views, criticisms, and thoughtful comments on the subject of time effectiveness; and to my many professional colleagues and the graduates of the Time Effectiveness workshops, for their encouraging me to put down in writing these questions and responses about time.

And finally, a special thanks to my family, without whose support, understanding, and cooperation the manuscript would never have been completed; to Ken, Eric, Douglas, Xenia, Marla, and their mother, Anneke—thank you.

R. R.

Contents

4   Getting a Grip on Time   77

5   Time Strategies   111

Just in Time
IMMEDIATE HELP FOR
THE TIME PRESSURED

Time Wasters: Confronting and Handling Them

There is one kind of robber whom the law does not strike at, and who steals what is most precious to men: time.

Napoleon I. *Maxims*

Time lost is time when we have not lived a full human life, time unenriched by experience, creative endeavor, enjoyment and suffering.

Dietrich Bonhoeffer, *Letters and Papers from Prison,* 1953

- ☐ I am very clear about what I want to do with my time.
- ☐ I often ask others, "What am I doing that wastes your time?"
- ☐ I am the cause of many of my own time wasters.
- ☐ Some time wasters are simply not worth the time and energy it would take to eliminate them.
- ☐ Most of my time wasters I have at least some control over.
- ☐ What might be considered a time waster by me might not be seen as a time waster by someone else.
- ☐ What might have been a good use of my time in the past may be an inappropriate use of my time now.
- ☐ I am able to distinguish a time waster (an inappropriate use of my time) from a time obligation (something I am obligated to do as part of my job or personal agreements).

We all waste time. Sometimes the reason is obvious. But often a time waster is only a symptom of a deeper problem, and treating the symptom will leave you pretty much where you were before the problem was even recognized: doomed to continue wasting time. The preceding checklist is designed to help you inventory your own understanding of how and why your time gets wasted and to point to some of the common underlying problems.

One way to view time is to imagine having a wheelbarrow filled with twenty-four hours. That twenty-four hours gets used one way or another, unfortunately too frequently by things that waste your time. The questions in this section deal with inappropriate uses of time, things that dump into your Wheelbarrow of Time. They also deal with how to confront and get control over these problems. Some of the insights you might find are a deeper understanding of what a time waster is and is not, how time wasters are created and who is responsible for them, and what some of those common time wasters that we all face in our daily lives are. The chapter outlines strategies for handling specific time wasters and avoiding some of the common but subtle traps in dealing with them.

---

1 What is a time waster? I am confused.

Defining a time waster may seem easy at first glance. A meeting, a telephone call, certain paperwork, the breakdown of the copy machine, social chitchat, and travel time may appear to be obvious time wasters. Yet when a serious effort is made to pinpoint the definition, real difficulty arises. To whom is the activity a time waster—to you or to someone else? When does it become a time waster—when the meeting runs past the adjournment time and is boring to you, when it doesn't start on time, or when the discussion isn't relevant to your needs?

To compound the problem, what's a waste of time for you or seen by you as a nonproductive use of your time may not necessarily be a waste for someone else, and what was a waste of time last month may be a good use of your time now, and vice versa.

Managers and professionals have variously described what they see as time wasters. For some, a time waster is an activity that takes time unnecessarily or uses time inappropriately. Others describe tasks that don't give a good return on time invested, or jobs they simply don't want to do.

One way to gain a comprehensive view of the time waster is to look at the characteristics common to all:

If you have perceived an activity to be a time waster, it is one for you—at least in your perception of it It may not be seen that way by others, but by you it is seen as a waste of time. You may consider the weekly Monday morning staff meeting a bore and a time waster, but your boss may think that it is an important, high-payoff activity (HIPO). Who is right? You perceive it to be a time waster; your manager perceives it to be a good use of time. The meeting may or may not be important, but that is not the question here. The critical point is that what you perceive as a time waster for you *is* a time waster for you, and it will remain one as long as you view it so.

All time wasters cause reactions Time wasters produce both physical and emotional reactions, and these can be either positive or negative. When you react in a positive, productive way, you enhance your chance to control the time waster and avoid losing more time in complaining and being upset over it.

All time wasters have a potential built-in time-waster multiplier That is, a negative reaction to a time waster may waste more time *after the fact* than the actual time waster did. For example, the ten minutes you were kept waiting for your boss to get off the phone can be multiplied in time by you. It is easy to convert this ten-minute wait into a thirty-minute gripe and moan session that your secretary and co-workers are forced to listen to. By then, you have tripled your own losses and wasted others' time, even though they couldn't do anything about your wasted time if their lives depended on it.

Every time waster is an inappropriate use of your time, by definition Yet some seem to be required by your job, such as that Monday morning staff meeting. First, though, look to see if, in fact, this activity you have defined as a time waster is a part of your job. If it is, then is it still a time waster? If it is, are you being paid to waste time? It may be more productive to see these activities not as time wasters but as time obligations— activities you are obliged to do. Many activities, such as filling out government forms, reviewing reports, disciplining subordinates, and listening to personal problems of your co-workers probably seem like time wasters. But they may be time obligations you have incurred in your role of manager, friend, or employee. If the time obligation seems like a waste of time, review your values and goals to see if your responsibility for this duty should and can be renegotiated.

All time wasters are caused—by you, others, or a combination of you and others To manage your time waster, you first need to determine who or what is causing it. If you think the time waster is caused by someone else, when actually it is caused by an invisible agreement, your own confusion over valued goals, or apathy, you will not be able to control it effectively. You will inappropriately attempt to shape up others while you are the one who must first shape up.

All time wasters provide negative "payoffs," which take the form of thoughts, feelings, and reactions Take the disorganized boss, for example. Ask yourself, "What do I get by having a disorganized boss who wastes my time?" Do you get to feel frustrated, angry, resentful, hurt, or demeaned? Do you get to think, "My boss is stupid. I could do a better job than that idiot." Perhaps you get to react in such a way that you get ulcers, and get to gripe and complain to others about how hard it is to have such a disorganized boss.

Even though such behavior is of course negative and nonproductive, for a variety of reasons people sometimes adopt it. It allows them to blame others instead of taking responsibility for getting their own work done. It also allows them to feel sorry for themselves and seek sympathy and condolences from their friends.

As long as these negative "payoffs" are more important to you than the positive rewards of getting rid of the time waster, you will do nothing about it.

All time wasters can be rationalized All time wasters can be blamed on someone else. That's easier than taking personal responsibility for them and either communicating your recommendations to someone who could do something about them or converting them into more productive activities.

You can always justify doing a time waster. You can say, "That is the way it is around here," or, "I'm just that way," or, "It's not my responsibility," or, "If they'd only get their act together, I wouldn't have to waste my time."

All time wasters make statements Listen to what they are saying to you. When your subordinates continually and inappropriately bring their problems to you to solve rather than solving them themselves, what does that say to you? When others misuse your time by continually imposing on your good will, what does that mean?

All time wasters can be replaced by more productive activities Time is wasted only when a higher payoff activity is being sacrificed. One key to winning the time game is to know exactly what you want to do with the time you free up when you eliminate a time waster; otherwise it will quickly be dominated by another low-payoff activity. The purpose of getting rid of the time waster is to replace it with an activity that is more valuable to you—whether it is spending time on planning or taking a walk. There are more worthwhile things to do in your work and life than you will ever have time to do, so replace the time waster with a more valuable activity.

All time wasters bear a cost/benefit ratio Although the benefits of eliminating a time waster usually clearly outweigh the costs (in terms of time, money, or energy), sometimes the opposite is true. For example, you could eliminate the time wasted by a senior staff member who insists on using his own filing system. As his boss, you could say, "Jack, your method is a waste of time. There are more important things I want you to do. The computer handles all this data now, quite nicely." But Jack may want to continue doing as he has done for the past thirty-five years. He will soon retire. The resentment and resistance Jack might feel (and the possible sabotage he could do) if you eliminated this unnecessary work isn't worth risking.

---

2 I have many time wasters. I wonder, could I possibly be partly responsible for them?

What happens to you and your time is almost always with your permission. Consciously or unconsciously, you have put your okay out to the world. When you realize that a time waster you thought was caused by others is really caused by you, ask yourself, "What is the invisible agreement that exists between the time waster and me that says it is okay?" Consider, for example, the co-worker who regularly comes into your office and chitchats when you have more pressing activities that you should be pursuing. What is the invisible agreement between you and the drop-in that says that it is okay, when in reality it isn't okay? In the case of the co-worker, the agreement might be:

It's okay to drop in on me and waste my time. I don't respect your time, so why should you respect mine?

I am always available. Call me your "open-door" friend.

It's okay, but we have to make it look like a business discussion.

It's okay, but I am going to get even with you later for doing this to me now.

It's okay, because I really didn't want to do what I was doing anyway, and now you have provided me with an excuse for not doing it.

Handling Invisible Agreements with Your Time Wasters

The first step in handling an invisible agreement is to be aware that you have one. You then can choose whether or not you want to do anything about it. Find out exactly how you feel about the invisible agreement and what you want to do about it. You may find that it's truly okay for it to be there and decide to let it be, or you may find that you want to eliminate or renegotiate it.

Acknowledging It and Accepting It

You may simply want to accept the invisible agreement rather than worrying or moving to do something about it. This could happen for several reasons. It may not be worth the pain, effort, time, or hassle to attempt to renegotiate the invisible agreement. You may find that although an activity wastes your time you like it too much to give it up—because it makes you feel important, gives you a sense of belonging, or allows you to avoid doing something that is more important but also riskier.

Renegotiation of the Invisible Agreement to Bring It into Alignment with Desired Goals

It is frequently necessary to renegotiate agreements, invisible and visible. The first step is to let other parties to the invisible agreement know your feelings and your intentions. Don't try to make them wrong so you can be right, but be sure they understand where you stand and what you want to see happen.

Invisible agreements, like any others, are of three general types: unilateral (an agreement only with yourself), bilateral (an agreement with one other person), and multilateral (an agreement with several other people).

Unilateral Agreement Negotiation   Unilateral agreements are agreements with yourself and can be renegotiated independently of others. If you have invisible agreements with yourself that it is okay for you to be preoccupied at work, do a slipshod job, and just get by, you may want to decide to renegotiate them. You may realize that you are allowing your time to pass without gaining real personal satisfaction or a sense of accomplishment. Draw up a contract with yourself—to participate more fully in your work; to put more of your skill, commitment, and energy into what you are doing; and to take advantage of the opportunities your work affords you to grow, develop, and make a worthwhile contribution.

Bilateral Agreement Negotiation   Here is an example of a bilateral agreement. Bryan had recently become upset over the fact that one of his co-workers, Ken, stopped to chitchat every time he walked by Bryan's office. Bryan felt this was, for the most part, an inappropriate and wasteful use of his time, but he didn't know what to do about it. When he looked for the invisible agreement, he realized he had conveyed to Ken the impression that he, Bryan, was the wise and experienced senior man around; that he was the nice guy who went out of his way to give assistance, the man who was always available to help, who really didn't have pressing matters to attend to, and whose time was anyone's who wanted to ask for it.

When Bryan discovered this invisible agreement, he realized that he had actually encouraged Ken, unconsciously, to drop in on him to chitchat. Bryan now saw that he had a choice to renegotiate the agreement. He let Ken know that he wanted to keep the friendship but that continual drop-in sessions were interfering with his work. Bryan suggested that they limit their conversations mostly to slack periods and coffee breaks so they would both have more time to concentrate on their work.

Bryan had now taken responsibility for his time and his agreement with Ken. He did this not by making Ken wrong and himself right, but in a way that kept Ken a friend and co-worker while still allowing Bryan more time to get his work done. He felt good about regaining some control over the time he had unknowingly relinquished to Ken through their invisible agreement.

Multilateral Agreement Negotiation   Diane was an assistant to a senior vice-president in her firm. This was a full-time, demanding job that took all of her time and energy. She was also responsible for supporting others in the office. She found herself continually asked by the vice-president and three other professional staff members to research reports, to make certain financial calculations, to gather data, and, in general, to do many activities that really prevented her from focusing on her responsibilities to the senior vice-president. Diane wanted to keep on being an effective team member, supporting the other members as much as possible, but she felt time-pressured and resentful about what she considered unfair demands on her time. She felt that many of these demands could be handled better by others if time were more effectively used in the office. She felt that most of what she was being asked to do by the vice-president and the three staff members she had not agreed to do at all. Diane was sure she faced an *A* time waster, that is, a time waster caused by others (as opposed to a *B* time waster, one caused by herself). Then, on further reflection, she began to see that, in fact, the time waster was not other-caused so much as self-caused. She looked at her invisible agreements and dicovered that she had unwittingly given the impression that "It's okay to ask me to research reports and do financial calculations, and to respond to your requests. I am a nice woman, I need the experience, and that's the reason I was hired." Right? Wrong.

Diane decided to take action to clean up this unworkable and negative invisible agreement. She sought out her immediate supervisor and got a clearer understanding of her role and responsibilities. This also let her define more sharply the high and low payoffs of her work as viewed by her principal scorekeeper, her boss. Further, she was able to renegotiate the time commitments, job responsibilities, and relationships at the office that had been based on other invisible agreements. Diane gained not only self-respect but also the support and respect of her co-workers.

Some days later, Diane found herself receiving such comments as:

"Gee, Diane, I didn't know that you felt so time-pressured and harried."

"Why didn't you tell us before that you felt we were dumping into your Wheelbarrow of Time? We could have worked out something long ago."

"I thought that this was part of your job, but now I see that others should have been handling it instead of you."

---

3 What are the most common time wasters mentioned by managers and what causes them?

Among the most common time wasters are:

Meetings	Conflicting priorities
Red tape	Waiting for others' work
Inability to say no	Poor delegation
Telephone calls	Office politics
Drop-ins	Incompetent staff
Bosses	Too much work
Paperwork	Attempting to do too much
Unclear organizational goals	Government agencies

This list could of course be much longer. Obviously, these items will not be time wasters in every case. The telephone, for example, can be a real time saver. Here, however, we are concerned only with that part of the activity which is perceived to waste time.

After recognizing something as a time waster, the next step is to determine its cause. How did it get to be a time waster, and who or what maintains it? I have added some time wasters to the list and sorted them all into two categories, *A* and *B*.

A	*B*
Meetings	Inability to say no
Red tape	Procrastination
Telephone calls	Disorganization
Bosses	Apathy

A	B
Paperwork	Routine tasks overdone
Unclear organizational goals	Failure to delegate
Drop-ins	Daydreaming
Conflicting priorities	Chip on shoulder
Incompetent staff	Poor relationship with boss

What's the difference between an *A* time waster and a *B* time waster? What characteristic distinguishes the *A*'s? What do the *B*'s have in common? It's very simple: The *A*'s are caused by outside forces or by other people, and the *B*'s are caused by ourselves. One executive described it this way: *A* time wasters are what they are doing to me, while *B*'s are what I am doing to myself.

Into which category do you think most executive time wasters fall? Most people choose *A*, since it's much easier to lay blame than to take responsibility for our own time. But in reality, practically all of the time wastes listed under *A* are in part, if not entirely, caused by ourselves. If you consider Monday's meeting a boring waster of time and yet continue to attend, you must accept some responsibility: you probably haven't clearly communicated your feelings to those who could do something about it. When you view a drop-in as a time waster, more often than not you have encouraged that person in some way to come in and chitchat with you.

We tend to blame others for our time wasters when in fact we are the ones who are most responsible for having them and for maintaining them.

As long as I am misidentifying the time wasters (that is, as long as I see them as *A*'s when in fact they are *B*'s), I can't effectively manage them, because I will be attempting to solve the problem by trying to shape up others when in fact I must first shape up myself.

One way for me to find out what the *B* is in those *A*'s is to ask myself the question, "What is the invisible agreement that I have with the time waster that allows it to be there?"

Seldom, if ever, will a group of individuals immediately recognize that their time wasters are caused not so much by others as by themselves. This is human, as it is easier, more pleasant, and more comfortable and ego-satisfying to believe that others are doing it to us, that others (whether boss, co-workers, spouse, or children) are really wasting our time. It is rough to admit to ourselves that we are our biggest time wasters, our biggest dumpers into our own personal Wheelbarrow of Time.

Yet there is good news in that realization, for if you are the problem then you are also the solution. You have incredible power to manage your time effectively, to get clear about what you want, to communicate to others clearly, and to negotiate and renegotiate agreements to enhance your sense of well-being.

4 How can I handle the many time pressures I face daily?

In the course of a normal day we make constant choices in our personal and professional lives about what to do with our time. We face all kinds of time demands, some clearly legitimate, some illegitimate and time-wasting. The following are strategies for handling time pressures and time wasters, questions to ask yourself when confronting your daily time dilemmas.

What Is the Real Problem?

Remember the adage "a problem well-defined is half solved"?
Define time pressures and time wasters as clearly and accurately as possible. Don't just say "people who drop in on me
and waste my time"—reduce generalities to specifics. *When* is
the drop-in a time waster? When you have other more
important things to do or when the person stays more than ten
minutes? Is it when the conversation strays from business to
personal matters? To whom is this activity a time waster, to you
or to someone else? Is this activity a good use of someone else's
time but not yours?

What Does Your Time Waster Tell You about the Way You Manage Your Time?

All time wasters make statements. When you take time to
listen, to train yourself to be open to what a time waster is
telling you, you will receive valuable information. See if you
can be a "neutral party"—stand back and tune in to what
messages are being sent. Does the time waster say:

"You have not been clear with others about what you really
expect of them"?

"You are personally so disorganized that you waste your own
time"?

"I am not really a time waster at all. I am part of your job, part
of your responsibilities"?

What Are Your Agreements Regarding the Time Pressure or Time Waster?

What agreements have you made regarding your time? With
whom did you make them—strictly with yourself or with
others? Are these agreements visible or invisible? How did they

become agreements, and what do you intend to do about them—do you want to keep them, renegotiate them, or eliminate them? For example, do you have an invisible agreement that says it is okay for others to dump into your Wheelbarrow of Time indiscriminately, that you will go along with it?

What Are the "Payoffs" of this Time Pressure/Time Problem?

Everything on which we spend time has its own particular payoffs—positive and negative. What are the payoffs for you in keeping this time pressure? Try to discover the "benefits" of keeping it. What are the negative "payoffs"? Do you get to feel angry, hassled, resentful? Do you get to complain to others who couldn't do anything about it even if their lives depended on it? Do you get to be a victim, feel sorry for yourself, and avoid doing what you are being paid to do because you "have to" spend so much time on time wasters? Take a moment and consider the genuine payoffs for gaining control over these same time pressures. Would you get to feel good about yourself? Would you gain the satisfaction of a job well done, for doing what you are being paid to do? Compare the payoffs for both keeping and ridding yourself of your time pressures/ time wasters. If the negative "payoffs" are more important to you than the positive payoffs of getting rid of the time problem, then you will do little if anything to solve the problem.

What Is the Source of the Time Pressure?

Determine the cause of the time problem. Is it caused by others, by some outside source, or is it caused entirely or primarily by you? A time problem can be, and often is, caused by a combination of other people and yourself. Often what seems to be a time waster caused by others is actually a time waster that you have caused yourself by your failure to take responsibility for your time, by your unawareness of what is happening with your time, or by your desire to be liked or feel busy.

How Am I Reacting to the Time Waster?

How do you view this problem? Do you react to it in ways that support you in confronting it and controlling it, or do you react in ways that make you upset, waste more time, and put added barriers between you and the effective use of your time?

---

5   I have trouble managing unwanted drop-ins. My office seems like Grand Central Station. What can I do?

You can categorize drop-ins into two broad groups: those you want to encourage and those you want to discourage. In either case, the following chart is designed as a mirror to reflect what would be useful and appropriate actions for you:

When...	*Then...*
Someone drops in on you,	Determine if it is a wanted or unwanted visit and determine who caused it, you or the other person.
It is not clear to you if it is a time waster or a legitimate demand on your time,	Distinguish the elements of the drop-in time that are legitimate and identify when

When...

Then...

the drop-in becomes a time waster. For instance, when five minutes or so of warm-up socializing extends inappropriately to twenty minutes, time is definitely wasted.

It is not clear how much time is needed for the meeting with the drop-in,

Set the "time space." Make an agreement on how much time is being allocated. When someone drops in on you at your office, you might say, "Steve, fine, I have twenty-five minutes; is that enough time for you?" When Steve answers, "Sure," then you have established the time space.

The conversation is dragging or drifting and not getting to the point,

Search for the reason behind the visit. You might say something like, "Steve, I sense that you are worried about the Davidson construction contract. Are you?" Steve might say, "No, but what I am concerned about is the way we are handling complaints from our contractors." You will have gotten to the point.

You feel the drop-in is not prepared for the discussion,

Suggest that, before taking both your time, Steve might first obtain the computer

When...

Then...

data from purchasing and talk with Marian in marketing. Get your drop-ins to do their homework before seeing you.

You feel that the drop-in is not leveling with you,

Level with the drop-in. Speak from your experience of the situation and, if appropriate, relate what you are feeling about what is happening. This will help get the drop-in's intentions and the appropriate considerations out on the table.

You know that you will have a particular drop-in for a discussion or to transact some sort of business,

Do your own homework. Have your secretary prepare a folder with pertinent data about the visitor and the business at hand. This will show that you respect the drop-in's time as well as your own. (This, of course, is even more essential when you have a scheduled visitor.)

There is an excessive number of unnecessary drop-ins that waste time and energy,

Check to see how *you* have helped initiate these visits. Try to see what your agreements and understandings are relative to sharing your time.

You have a chronic drop-in who is wasting your time,

Have a script prepared to deal with the problem the next time the drop-in comes by.

When...	*Then...*
Your subordinates are passing unwanted tasks to you,	Understand that you are foolish for taking them. Clarify your agreements and determine whose problem is whose.
You are not sure what you want to do about certain drop-ins or how you want to handle them,	Look at your agreements with them. Check out your real intentions—not what you would like to do or what would be nice to do, but what you really intend to do. What commitments are you willing to make in order to handle the drop-in?
The physical arrangement of your office encourages the wrong kind of drop-in or encourages drop-ins to stay too long,	Arrange your office furniture and space to support your purposes. If chairs are too comfortable, you may want to change them. Do you have books, models, pictures, or other artifacts that are causing you to waste time or others to linger? (Some of these items can be supportive of good time management by facilitating conversation, building a working relationship, or putting people at ease.)
You would like to let the drop-in know that you want to finish soon,	Initiate a closing, such as, "Before I let you go ...," or, "Before we wrap it up, I wonder, have we covered what you wanted to cover?"

When...	*Then...*
You want to get an insistent drop-in to leave your office,	Be firm with your closing technique. You might say, "I am going to let you go because I know that you are very busy, and I have to get back to my work, too." It is important that you time it right and are courteous but firm. When you respect your own and others' time, terminating your get-together becomes a mere formality— polite and almost automatic.

---

6 I have difficulty distinguishing a true time waster from a time obligation. Are there any guidelines?

Time wasters are those activities that you feel waste your time, dump into your Wheelbarrow of Time, or are inappropriate uses of your time. They are activities you want to eliminate or, at the minimum, reduce in negative impact.

There is another group of activities that, at first glance, may seem like time wasters but are not. These are time obligations arising from your personal working relationships, which remain legitimate until the agreements (to perform certain tasks, take on certain responsibilities, perform in certain ways) are changed.

Is attending a chamber of commerce meeting as your organization's representative a time waster or a time obligation? What about spending time with a subordinate reviewing past performance or filling out required union forms or attending staff meetings? What about listening to the problems of co-workers or covering for your boss when he has failed to complete his work properly? The answer isn't always clear.

A time waster you move to eliminate; a time obligation you move to turn to your advantage by making the time spent on it more rewarding. The following is a good example of what is meant.

One highly successful executive, pressed by the demands of his growing firm to work long hours and often on weekends, tried to make it up to his fourteen-year-old son by agreeing to go on a scout campout. He drove to the campsite, tired and cranky, after a particularly hectic week, feeling guilty about the things he was neglecting at the office and terribly resentful of the other fathers who hadn't volunteered to come. But he caught himself in mid-thought. He was coming to help the boys on their Eagle Scout requirements—something that was very important to them. He had freely agreed to do so. So he asked himself how he could turn his time obligation to his advantage, to make it enhance his life or his contribution to a valued goal.

The answer he arrived at was to abandon his negative attitude and to view the outing as an opportunity to really be with his son on the scouting program. He decided to spend the time with the troop teaching, learning, and relaxing. Consequently, he found himself enjoying his son and the other boys, renewing his enthusiasm for the outdoors, and feeling proud of his contribution to scouting. He converted a time obligation (incurred because he had agreed to be at the outing) to his advantage and to the advantage of his son and the scout troop.

Look at your own list of time wasters. How many are really time obligations? How many are part of a game or role you have chosen to play, such as employee, friend, co-worker, manager, parent, or spouse? Ask yourself whether you're being paid to handle the task and if it is part of what you have implicitly or explicitly agreed to do. If the answer is yes, the chances are it is not a time waster, at least not in the eyes of your scorekeepers—your boss, organization, client, or family.

If it is a time obligation:

- Find ways to turn it to your advantage and, of course, to the advantage of your organization.
- Look for the real value of the activity and take responsibility for getting it done.
- Reassess the task periodically to make sure that it's still necessary.
- Renegotiate your agreements to get rid of the obligation, if appropriate.

Look repeatedly at your activities, and ask yourself, "Do I really need to do this?" Here are some alternatives if a task turns out to be a time waster:

- Find ways either to eliminate it or to cut your losses and get on with your job.
- Look for the invisible agreements (unspoken understandings) that legitimize it, and renegotiate them.
- Take total responsibility for knowing that it is a time waster. If appropriate (and it almost always is), tell someone who can do something about it.
- Recognize who caused it (others, yourself, or both), figure out what you are doing to maintain it, and then move to change it.

As you move to convert a time obligation to your advantage and make it a higher payoff, you may face certain barriers like the following.

Still thinking of it as a time waster   As long as you have this attitude, it will be nearly impossible to turn the obligation to your advantage. You must be able to see it as an opportunity for enhancing your life.

Resenting having to do it   Resentment can trap you into feeling sorry for yourself and sabotage your efforts to increase the value of this activity, for you and for your organization.

Not liking doing it   Go back and check the task against your valued goals, your agreements, and the roles you play. Why don't you like it.? Is it too difficult? Does it go against your better judgment? Is it distasteful? Are there other things you would rather do? Until an obligation is acceptable, you won't be able to make it pay off.

Not being sure how to turn it to your advantage   Seek assistance in this. Ask your scorekeepers how they see it. Find out how others have handled similar situations.

Again, when an activity is a time waster, move to eliminate it. And when an activity is a time obligation move to convert it to your advantage. The difference between an inappropriate use of your time and a time obligation is not always clear. Ask yourself, "Is doing this activity required by understandings I have with myself and others?" If so, at least for the present, it is a time obligation—one that supports an agreement and/ or role responsibility that you have. If it is an activity that does not support an agreement or role responsibility and does not make your life better for you, it is a time waster.

---

7   I spend my time on time wasters that don't seem worth eliminating. Am I kidding myself?

There will be times when you decide not to try to eliminate a time waster because it would cost too much to eliminate it. You may run up against a longstanding institutional or company policy, for example, that all interoffice memos are to be typed in triplicate—one sent to the department head, one kept in central filing, and the other kept for your files. It may be faster and more efficient simply to make notations on the reports and send them on, but your boss may want it done a certain way. After testing the possibility of eliminating this activity, you may decide there would be resistance (even animosity) to any change, and it may not be worth the effort. So you cut your losses: do a minimum acceptable level of performance and get on with your work.

Are you kidding yourself? You can find out by checking out your reasons for not eliminating the time waster. Is it truly because the cost is too great, or are there other less valid reasons? These may be getting in the way of your desired result. The list of reasons (excuses), such as, "I will do it later," or, "It really doesn't waste that much time," or, "No one really cares," or, "I can't do anything about it," is nearly endless.

Are you really fooling yourself or have you made an honest and clear evaluation of the situation and determined that the cost is too high to eliminate this particular time-wasting activity?

---

8   I am easily distracted and lose concentration, which causes me to waste time. What can I do?

Distractions break concentration, cause loss of momentum, and take us down paths that are unproductive. The key to controlling time is focusing on what needs to be done, giving it your full attention and commitment. Here are some common contributors to feeling distracted:

Your desk is so messy or stacked so high it qualifies for the next archeological dig

- Instruct your secretary on how your desk "works," how you want it to be managed. Ask her for suggestions and then get agreement and let her act as a monitor to screen out unnecessary paperwork.
- Get off the route list of unnecessary magazines, reports, statistical materials, and division memos.
- Dump as much of the material on your desk as possible into the wastebasket.
- Commit yourself to an orderly desk, one that minimizes the chance of causing you distraction. It is so easy to see a report in your left-hand pile of paper, or get curious about some statistical computer runs, or be distracted by a picture of your loved ones. There certainly is a place for pictures, favorite objects, trophies, and photographs, but when they are distractions, it is not on your desk.

You seem to have little power of concentration Lack of concentration is selective. While you may not be able to concentrate on completing your written recommendation to management, you may be so concentrated while viewing a movie that a bomb could be placed next to you without your knowing it. Work to expand your power of concentration, in areas that really matter to you.

- When you find an intruding thought breaking your concentration, don't fight it. Acknowledge that it is there, and then let it go and return immediately to the task at hand. In this way you avoid the tension and frustration of resisting the intruding thought, which, of course, is impossible anyway.
- State an affirmation: "I am fully capable and desire to concentrate 100 percent on this task." An affirmation is a

positive, here and now statement about a condition you want to reinforce. Send this affirming message to your mind.

- Develop a concentrating self-esteem. Visualize yourself as an individual with incredible powers of concentration. This visualization and affirmation will support increased concentration.
- Realign your thinking to focus as long as possible on one subject. If you are able to focus on writing without interrupting yourself for only five minutes, then work to extend this to ten minutes. Reward yourself immediately when you have extended your power of concentration. Often the only reward that you will need is the reward of increased productivity and a sense of self-mastery over preoccupation and lack of focus.

You jump from one task to another haphazardly

- Work for completeness. Focus on one thing at a time. Visualize the appropriate completion of the activity you have just started. See yourself completing it. Imagine how it would feel to have so completely focused on this activity.
- Tackle one thing at a time. Tackle first things first when you find yourself inundated with problems or deadlines.
- Set a minimum time that you will work on a task. If you are at your desk, during this time don't get out of your chair to get a drink, go to the bathroom, or do any other activity. Even if you do nothing, stay in that seat for the agreed amount of time.

Create an environment that helps you combat distraction. Keeping a tidy, nondistracting desk was mentioned earlier. Expand this to your total work area. Look for things that you can change or remove, like distracting furniture or decor. Note what gets you off focus and then move to eliminate as many of these things as possible.

Consider taking a course in concentration or meditation. You have a unique and incalculably powerful mind for focusing and concentrating. Capture this power and put it to use.

---

9   It seems that I waste a lot of time and energy on time wasters that are unavoidable. How can I prevent this?

If you truly cannot do anything about a time waster, if you have no real control over it, then acknowledge this and accept it as something that (at least right now) you have to live with. But remember that the problem in wasting time is not so much the actual time waster—for example, the fifteen minutes you waste waiting for your boss to get off the phone or the thirty minutes that is wasted in a required but totally irrelevant meeting. The real trouble is that you can easily waste much more time by moaning and complaining about it to others.

By doing this you not only waste your own time and energy by getting angry and resentful, but you often waste others' time as well. Then what was initially fifteen misspent minutes becomes an additional thirty-minute time waste because of the way you choose to react to it. In fact, more time is usually wasted after the fact than was wasted on the time waster itself—in anger, upset, complaining to others, or getting even.

In the physical world, for every action there is an equal and opposite reaction. By analogy, we can say that for every action that is directed toward you, you have a reaction. Here is an example. You are given a job that is clearly a waste of your time: you have to redo an assignment that wasn't done correctly in the first place by one of your co-workers. Certainly, it may be appropriate to confront the person who failed to do the assignment correctly, to prevent or minimize the possibility of its happening again. But you also have a choice about how you will personally react to this action, and the way you choose to react will largely determine how much additional time you waste on the project. You can get angry, frustrated, or resentful that the person is so stupid and can't seem to get anything done right. You can blame others, complain, and get so upset that you have to go home for the rest of the day. Or, you can choose to react in ways that minimize the time wasted, in ways that support your purpose and get your job done.

Here is a poem, author unknown, that illustrates this action-reaction phenomenon. The poem is called "Stepping Stone or Stumbling Blocks" and talks about the ways you and I can handle what happens to us in life—either as a stumbling block or a stepping stone.

> Isn't it strange that princes and kings
>   and clowns that caper in sawdust rings
> And common folk like you and me
>   are builders for eternity
>
> To each is given a book of rules
> A block of stone and a bag of tools
> For each must shape ere time has flown
> A stumbling block or a stepping stone.

There will be times when you will unfairly be required to do something, when your time will be wasted by people not doing their jobs right, or when you will be asked for data that you know no one will ever look at. These events are inappropriate uses of your time, but they are still there for you to handle. That is the reality of your time.

As the poem describes, each of us must "shape ere time has flown/a stumbling block or a stepping stone." We can either react to these time wasters in such a way that we stumble all over them, getting resentful, upset, or even causing ulcers for ourselves, or we can use them as stepping stones to make our lives better.

How can we use time wasters? Ask yourself the question, "What can I learn from this time waster?" Legitimate uses of your time may take on more meaning, especially when compared to the time-wasting activities that you sometimes have to spend time on. After you have handled it, reflect on what you have learned for handling similar situations.

It is your choice how to react to time wasters. You can either control them and cut your losses on them or you can handle them in a way that makes them true stumbling blocks for you, wasting more time and making your work and life more difficult for you. It's your choice.

Realities of Time

This Time like all times is a very good one if we but know what to do with it.

Ralph Waldo Emerson

Our costliest expenditure is Time.

Theophrastus (370–287 B.C.)

One of these days is none of these days.

English Proverb

☐ Even if I were managing my time well, I wouldn't be able to do everything I want to do.

☐ I know what my valued goals are.

☐ I know where my time goes.

☐ I am aware of the invisible (implied) agreements that determine how some of my time is spent.

☐ I consider time to be one of my most valuable resources.

☐ My significant others are aware of what my goals are.

Is there really as much time as you think there is? How much control do you really have over it? What are the givens of your time "equation," the realities of time that you must work with? In order to understand the hows and whys of your time pressures, you must first understand something about the nature of time.

The few simple truths contained in this chapter (and hinted at in the preceding checklist) can be used as basic tools for gaining control of a time-pressured life—a solid foundation on which to build your time strategies.

10 If I manage my time effectively, will I find enough time to do all the important things I want to do?

No, there is never enough time to do everything. Even if given 400 lifetimes, we wouldn't have enough time to do all the valuable things we would like to do. Most people would like to have more time to travel, to study, to write, to spend with loved ones, more time to spend on community projects, to pursue hobbies, to read, to exercise, or to search out new areas of life and career interests. Many of us would like to take more time to find out what we would really like to spend our time on, but we don't even do this as we would like because we are so busy.

There is never enough time to do all that is worthwhile and important. Ask yourself, "What are some of the implications of this scarcity of time for me—as a person, as a manager, as a member of my community, as a parent or friend?" Among them might be the following:

· I must acknowledge more completely the importance of placing priorities on my activities.
· I must look at my personal and work goals and select those goals that are most important. For those, I want to provide work time. I also need to identify the selected activities that will best help me accomplish these goals.
· I must be aware that while each choice I make opens doors to new opportunities, it also precludes others. Therefore, I must make my choices carefully.
· I am reminded that I am not superhuman, that I am, in fact, mortal.

Knowing that there is only a limited amount of time helps support my effort to be 100 percent responsible for the way I choose to use my personal and work time.

---

11 Why don't I ever have enough time? It seems like every time I get caught up, more work is thrown at me—I never catch up.

This is a feeling most of us have more often than we might like to admit. Just as there is never enough time to do all the important things in your personal life, the same probably holds true for your job. What do you do?

1 Acknowledge that there is never enough time to do everything important. That is neither good nor bad; it is not a value statement. It is simply true.

2 Understand also that there is not enough time to do all the low-payoff, inconsequential things vying for your attention.

3 Actively and firmly establish the parameters of your goodwill, the limits of your willingness to spend time on doing things. This includes clarifying your agreements about what you can and cannot do with yourself and others.

4 Know that your boss, spouse, children, and friends are not clairvoyant. It may be that they just don't know that you are over your head and out of time.

5 Be responsible and communicate to your boss (or significant others) that, since there isn't enough time to do

everything, some decisions about priorities are going to have to be made.

6 Run a time inventory to see just how much time things are taking. Do this not just for your evaluation but also for review by your significant others.

7 Estimate how much time you would need to do all things that come across your desk. Is it even possible to complete them in the time you are given? (You might find that you need twenty-eight hours in the day to finish them.)

8 Constantly look for ways to eliminate some of the work you are now doing, to streamline it, and to reduce the time you spend on certain parts of it. Find ways to reduce the overt perfectionism in your work without substantially affecting its effectiveness. Look for tasks you can delegate to others.

9 Establish the parameters of your willingness to take on additional work.

10 Ask for help from your significant others, be they co-workers, subordinates, or your boss. Document where your time is going, the problems as you see them, and any ideas for solutions that you might have.

---

12   I realize that there will never be enough time to do everything that I would like to do. My question is how do I use this information?

The realization that there is never enough time has different messages for different people. Ask several friends what it means to them and you will receive as many different feelings and responses as people you question. Here is a variety of responses:

I have to live a selective life, spending time on those activities that support most fully my valued goals.

Knowing that I have limited time and will never do all the important things in life helps me establish the boundaries of my goodwill. I now can say no to worthwhile requests on my time, simply because I acknowledge that there is never enough time. I now know that when I say no to these kinds of requests I am not saying, "No, it is not worthwhile and important for me to do"; I am saying no because I acknowledge that there is never enough time for everything.

This awareness of the scarcity of time reminds me to stop every once in a while and ask, "Is this the best use of my time right now?" Time is precious, always in constant, limited supply, and I am responsible for the management and husbandry of it.

It helps me appreciate the time I do have. I know that it is a gift, that all things happen in time, and that I can't afford to allow people and circumstances to indiscriminately waste it.

I know that I have no more and no less time than anyone else. Some choose to use their time in ways that support them and enhance their happiness and sense of well-being. Others don't. The choice is up to me to use my time well.

Knowing that there is never enough time emphasizes, I hope in a positive way, that I am mortal and that I have no guarantee how long I will be on this earth. To manage my time in a way that is productive, fulfilling, and contributive is an opportunity that I have as a responsible human being.

You may want to take a few moments to reflect on what
"there is never enough time for all the worthwhile and
important things in life" means to you.

---

13 I have heard that it is important to become aware of illusions in managing our time. What does that mean?

An illusion is something that deceives or misleads. When you
have an illusion, your clouded perception causes you to
misinterpret the actual nature of what you're seeing. For
example, if you are under the illusion that you are using your
time effectively (when actually you are not), you cannot do
anything about it because the illusion blinds you to the fact that
there is a problem. You can't change this until you discover the
illusion for yourself. So first recognize an illusion for what it
is—a false reality. Then look beyond this false reality to a more
accurate picture of reality.

One common illusion in managing time is that you think
you know where your time goes, when in fact you don't. Unless
you have made a time review or study, the chances are almost
100 percent that you don't know how you spend your time.
And if you do know where your time is going, you most likely
are midjudging the value of the time you spend—unless you
have given it serious thought. Make a personal time study, not
only to determine where the time goes, but also to determine
how you feel about the way it is being used. A time study helps
you to overcome the illusion that you know what you are doing
with your time.

Another common illusion in managing time is to think you are being *effective* (doing the right job right) when actually you are only being *efficient* (doing the job right, but not necessarily the right job). Perhaps you're still working on computer reports that were necessary last month but are no longer needed because the problems that generated the report have been solved. The computer still keeps spewing forth data that are no longer needed.

Or maybe you are still filling out data for old organizational reports that are no longer necessary—efficiently, meticulously, and ineffectively filling them out. You may be working under the illusion that these kinds of activities need to be done because they were once legitimate demands on your time. Yet they are not needed now.

Dealing with these and other illusions that impair effective time use is a central theme of this book. We must pierce these illusions to begin working with the realities of our time and life. Once we understand how frequently we deceive ourselves, a major step toward personal and professional time effectiveness has been taken.

---

14 Why do I have so many time pressures? I am sure that these problems say something to me, but I am not sure what.

Awareness is one of the basic keys to managing your time effectively, and every one of your time pressures has something to tell you if you will only listen to its message. Regardless of what they are—more to do than you can possibly do, conflicts between personal and business life, repeated postponement of important tasks, or inordinate demands on your time—your individual time pressures are all telling you something important.

Take, for example, the problem of having more to do at work or at home than you have time for. You may feel hassled, harried, hurried, resentful, and frustrated. What can you do? First, listen to what the situation is telling you. It could be saying any of the following:

- You are trying to do too many things.
- You need to learn how to say no more effectively.
- You have a neurotic need to feel busy (or to feel guilty).
- You have not properly determined your valued goals and their corresponding priorities and payoffs.
- You are too disorganized to get much done.
- You purposely take on more than you can do in order to feel victimized.
- You like to be busy because it's a good excuse for not getting the really important things done.

The message provided by your time pressure tells you what you need to do about it. People concerned about time often ask what they should do about a particular time problem. But answers are of little help unless the cause of the pressure is understood, because how you deal with the problem will be determined by the source of the pressure.

No gimmicks or techniques or strategies will help you until you are aware of why you are pressured.

The next time you want to confront a time pressure, take a moment to define it (boring meeting, broken appointment, drop-in visitor) and then in a quiet, relaxed place close your eyes and submerge yourself in it. Feel it, look at it, live with it, take note of all the feelings it prompts. Ask your time problem questions, talk to it, and let it talk to you. Does this sound strange? Do it and see the value of taking time to listen and becoming more aware of what is really happening with your time.

---

15 Why does my time seem to have so many demands on it that I can't find time to do the things that I really want to do?

Your time gets mortgaged and committed by the agreements you make. These agreements may be visible and conscious, or they may be more subtle—invisible and unrecognized by you. For example, there may be a visible agreement that your regular Tuesday morning meetings begin at 9:00. But the invisible, binding agreement is that you, as chairman of the meeting, will wait until the last person gets there (which is almost always 9:20 or 9:25) to start the meeting. Often the invisible agreement works to nullify the visible one.

Your time is also demanded by games or roles you have committed yourself to play. Being an employee of an organization is one game or role you play that makes it necessary, if you are going to play by the rules of the game, to account for your time to others—your manager, co-workers, clients. Other roles that may impact on your time and mortgage it (most likely in a positive, satisfying, and productive way) are those of spouse, parent, friend, or member of your church and community. Awareness that your time is mortgaged to the extent of your agreements and the games or roles that you play provides real choices about how to manage your time.

If you do not like how your time gets used at work or at home, look at the agreements and understandings you have that have created this situation. Analyze the various roles and games you play. You may find that you want to change some agreements or discontinue some of the roles and games you are playing. Certainly some will be more difficult to change than others, but paying close attention to the understandings, invisible agreements, and roles that you are involved in will increase your time effectiveness even if you must keep on playing them.

Understanding that your time gets mortgaged because of your commitments gives you some clear options. As you make choices and agreements now and in the future, you can choose more carefully what you agree to do and what role or game you choose to play. You may want to seek out time commitments more directly, in order to find roles and agreements that support your well-being, enhance your sense of accomplishment, and improve the quality of your life. You will know clearly that your agreements and roles all use one of your most precious resources: time.

Remember, there is never enough time to do all the worthwhile and valuable things in life. Time is precious, choices must be made, and you are subject to the law of mortgaged time: *your time is called upon and mortgaged to the extent you have entered into agreements, understandings, and roles or games in your life.* Taking responsibility for the quality of the agreements and games you play enhances the quality of your time and life.

---

16 Isn't time management really just common sense?

In many ways, yes, but common sense that is not often practiced. How many times have you done a stupid thing? If you are at all like me, many times. How many times have you done something stupid and known it was stupid when you did it, and then done it again? We all belong to the same club: we just don't always use our common sense. In fact, there are some cynics who say that there is nothing so uncommon.

It is common sense to know what you value and want out of life   Yet for many this is one of the primary deferred high payoffs. The clarification of what you truly value as a human being, as a parent, or as an executive who has reached the top of your organization is fundamental; but it is also easily postponable to the more pressing, urgent matters of the day. The phones are ringing, you have to attend an important meeting, there are conflicts to be resolved, piles of paperwork to do, places to go, people to see—there's no time now.

People often say, "I know that it is a high payoff for me to determine what I really value, and I am going to do it—later." Later too often means "whenever"—whenever I get a chance to get around to it, when the pressure stops, when I get motivated, when the telephone stops ringing, when I stop getting requests to do this and that from by boss, subordinates, spouse, and children. But the real meaning of "whenever" is "never."

It is common sense to know how to use your time   Before you can manage your time effectively, you need to know how you are using it. This is only common sense, but it is seldom practiced. Many of us assume that we know how we use our time. But in fact it is nearly impossible to assess your time accurately unless you periodically make some kind of a time study. Do you know how much time you spend unnecessarily in stop-start efforts, correcting miscommunications, or handling daily interruptions? Is excessive time in chitchat and social conversation being interpreted as "team building"? Or is time wasted in preoccupation and fuzzy thinking being labeled "creative thinking" time?

In addition, time does not always move at the same pace psychologically: sometimes it passes quickly and at other times it drags. This is another reason making it very difficult for you to know your time and how you are using it, unless you periodically make some kind of time audit.

It is common sense to value time Time is a most precious resource: limited, nonrefundable, and the arena in which everything takes place. It is common sense to protect it, guard it, and use it as one of your most precious commodities. But observe how time is squandered, allowed to dribble and trickle away in meaningless and foolish ways, and treated as a limitless, valueless commodity. How consistently do you practice valuing time?

It is common sense to organize time Time, like any other valuable resource, needs to be organized to gain desired results, to obtain a balance between the important but not urgent tasks and the urgent but not important tasks. That is, time needs to be structured in ways that support making time for the high-payoff activities as well as for the necessary, low-payoff tasks. Even though this is common sense, it is often not done. If many of us organized and managed our money as poorly as we do our time, personal and organizational bankruptcy would be far more common.

It is common sense to plan time Planning is charting the road map for the future. Common sense dictates that you know where you want to go, and plan and develop the means to get you there.

But planning for most is a deferred activity, postponed in the face of real or imagined crises and preoccupation with the unimportant low payoffs and immediate pressures of the day. Planning is recognized as important but seldom seen as urgent. It is something that we are going to do later, when we have more time, when it isn't so hectic and busy, when we can devote our fully energy and time to it. But "later," as mentioned before, usually translates as "never."

It is common sense to take action   If important tasks are to be accomplished and values are to be implemented, action must take place on those activities that make the difference. Initiative must be taken to actualize valued goals. Have you observed how some constantly play the waiting game, waiting for something miraculous and wonderful to happen to them so that they get to play the game of life, to get what they want? Winning the time game dictates that you take responsibility for making the important and high-payoff things happen in your life and your professional career.

It is common sense to give time to the truly important and high-payoff activities in our lives. It is common sense that unfortunately for so many isn't practiced.

Know what you value, know how you use your time. Value that time, plan and organize it in ways that support your valued goals. Take positive actions that are aligned with your valued and personal and professional goals. Then you will certainly be practicing the art of common sense in time management.

But time management isn't just common sense, at least if we define it as something consistently practiced all or most of the time by most of us. It is only common sense when it is practiced. And the more that you practice common sense in your time management, the more effectively you will use your time and enhance your personal and professional effectiveness.

Payoffs and Priorities: A Critical Difference in Time

Real generosity toward the future lies in giving all to the present.

Albert Camus, *The Rebel,* 1951

If I want something to happen, I must make time and space for it.

Time Effectiveness Workshop participant

☐ I usually give high-payoff activities high priority.
☐ I review and reassess my goals regularly.
☐ I make a daily list of priorities.
☐ I set aside special time for important activities such as planning.
☐ High-payoff activities are easy to postpone.
☐ I have a great deal of choice in how I manage my time.
☐ I regularly assess the value of what I am doing.

A major challenge in playing the time game is to align your payoffs and priorities—that is, to know how to give time to the activities that are truly rewarding. For most of us the relationship is not automatic. We may find ourselves spending hours doing some unnecessary task (and doing it perfectly), while an extremely important activity gets shortchanged. We continually put off finding time to plan, time to begin a promising new project, and even time to spend with the people we love. High priorities are placed on routine matters, while some of the lowest payoff activities dominate much of our time.

The key to aligning payoffs and priorities is a clear understanding of goals and values. For if we haven't taken time to determine what is truly important to us, we will have a hard time knowing what even deserves our time.

The questions and answers in this chapter deal with the problems of recognizing and making time for high payoffs

(HIPOs) and guarding against the domination of low-payoff (LOPO) activities.

---

17 Why do I often postpone important and high-payoff activities such as planning and spending time with my family?

There could be many reasons for this. Clearly, one reason is that high-payoff activities (HIPOs), such as those you mention, have certain characteristics that make them seem postponable in relation to more immediate matters.

High-payoff activities are frequently cloudy and not well defined What does it mean to "clear up an agreement," to "express love to someone," or to find "time to think"? Activities that positively contribute to a valued goal may not be defined concretely in our minds. The clearer you can be about what specifically *does* contribute, the better your chances of finding time for it. It is very difficult to find time to do something nonspecific, even if you have the time to do it.

High-payoff activities do not seem urgent Seldom, if ever, do these HIPOs have deadlines. Planning, clearing up your anger and resentment with someone, and establishing your personal values are all easily deferable until tomorrow when you are not so busy. In a sense, it is never urgent that you be a loving parent or that you determine what your values are. The chances are strong that unless you motivate yourself to make time for these activities, they will continue to be deferred.

No one can really make you do your high payoffs   Since they do not seem urgent, you are the one who must take the initiative and make it a high priority to give time to these important concerns. Clearly, no one in the world can make you be a loving parent or a loving person. You and you alone decide if you're going to make this a high priority. Certainly there will often be people and events that will encourage you, but you and you alone are the one who must decide to act on the deferred high payoff.

High-payoff activities are not critical to maintaining the status quo   Therefore, you can continue to do what you are now doing without ever activating any of your high-payoff activities. In fact, the status quo will change only when you make time to incorporate these HIPOs into your life. Are you willing to chance changing the way things are now, in anticipation that things will be better?

The rewards and penalties for failing to do these important, potentially high-payoff activities are sometimes not clear. It may be difficult to imagine what the actual rewards are for finding time to spend with your family, making time for creative planning, or clearing up your agreements with your partner. Certainly the penalties are often obscured until it is too late to do anything about them. Many parents have found their child grown, no longer that little boy they once knew, and said, "I wish that I had spent more time with him. I was always too busy, and now it is too late." Similarly, not making time for creative and essential planning for either your professional or personal life can backfire. You may find yourself confronted with problems that could have been solved easily with some forethought.

Being too busy to plan can turn into a long-term liability that the short-term asset of saved time can't justify. The penalty for not establishing your values—the loss of joy and satisfaction of what might have been if you had—may come too late to correct the situation. But, then again, you may wake up just in time.

---

18 Why do I waste so much time on activities that are low-payoff, trivial, and possibly even unnecessary?

This is a very common time problem. The following factors may give you insight into why this happens.

You may not be aware that you have some real choices in the management of your time You can choose to stop doing some time-consuming and low-payoff activities completely, without adversely affecting your work or personal life. In fact, conscientiously stopping some of your unnecessary low pay-offs frees up time to spend more wisely on higher-payoff tasks.

You may lack clear, purposeful, viable goals To have a sense of accomplishment, you need a standard or goal against which to measure your progress. Clear, practical goals can enhance your ability to protect your time against the encroachment of LOPO (low-payoff) dominance. When you don't have a goal, when you don't know where you want to go or be, it is easy to be dominated by unnecessary or marginal low-payoff activities.

You may be a prisoner of your past and continue to do low-payoff activities simply because you have always done them Perhaps at one time they were legitimate demands on your time. Perhaps your goals have changed but your activities have not; that is, you may have failed to initiate new activities to support your new goals. Perhaps a particular activity used to be required by your organization, your boss, or someone else but no longer is. The ways of being trapped in the past are many.

You may be taking the path of least resistance   Many a city street in our country winds and turns as it does because it was once a cowpath that led to the water hole. Similarly, many people fall victim to doing particular things simply because they are the easiest things to do. Low-payoff activities are often easy to do. Doing them requires no great personal risk, rocks no boats, and is not demanding.

The longer you follow the path of least resistance, the more difficult it becomes for you to chart new ground, take more responsible control over your life, and do what will give you a greater sense of accomplishment and well-being.

You may feel that you "have to" do all these low-payoff activities   Many LOPOs are necessary and even, at times, urgent to do (completing certain forms in time for audit, filing, answering the telephone), but some are unnecessary and should be eliminated.

You may need to feel busy, wanted, or victimized by your LOPOs   Low-payoff activities may help you look important or give you a feeling of accomplishment. Routine and trivial (but time-consuming) activities may be an excuse to justify to yourself and others why you can't find time for important, but possibly risky and difficult, high payoffs in your work and life.

You may have relinquished too much control of your time to others   There are people who have nothing better to do than to think of dumb LOPOs for you to do—and since you are dumb enough to do them, it boggles their minds and encourages them to go back to their LOPO drafting boards to think of more dumb LOPOs for you to do. These people come in many different shapes and sizes; they often are bosses, co-workers, youngsters, next-door neighbors, friends, spouses, or subordinates.

You may have failed to build a self-destruct mechanism into your LOPOs Many activities that waste time (or shouldn't even be done now) are done because there is no built-in system to terminate the activity when it becomes obsolete. Many a committee, computer report, office procedure, report, or requirement continues long after any real purpose is served. It is too bad activities aren't like "mission impossible" tapes, automatically self-destructing when their useful lives are over.

Your time is well spent in clarifying the reasons you have created for spending and wasting so much time on the LOPOs of your work and life, at the sacrifice of higher-payoff activities. You have enormous control over choices and decisions you make about yourself and your time.

You can be assured of one thing: if you are wasting time on LOPOs when there is much to be done that would be more satisfying to you, you and you alone are responsible for deciding what to do about it. No one will come to your rescue and make you do those things that bring joy, give a sense of accomplishment, or enhance your self-esteem.

---

19 How can I separate the necessary low-payoff activities from those activities that no longer need to be done?

There is little doubt that all of us spend valuable time on certain low-payoff activities that no longer are legitimate uses of our time. These activities that should not be done need to be ferreted out from among the appropriate and legitimate activities you do. You can begin to separate the necessary from the unnecessary by using the following strategies. They do not have to be followed in the exact order presented. You also may find that one strategy is more appropriate or helpful than another.

Ask yourself the following questions:

When Will I Stop Doing This Activity?

When, for example, am I going to stop reading every magazine, report, and piece of written material that reaches my desk? When am I going to stop having unproductive and boring staff meetings that are no longer needed? When am I going to stop making two or three rough drafts when the first draft is good enough? Put each activity that you do on "trial" for its life. Does it still seem to be a legitimate use of your time?

Why Am I Doing This?

When you suspect that you are facing an unnecessary and time-consuming activity, ask yourself, "Why am I doing this when I feel no one wants it done anyway? Who says it is necessary for me to do it? What purpose does it serve?"

How Does This Activity Make a Contribution to Valued Goals?

What contribution does this activity make to a personal, team, management, or organizational goal? If you can't determine how any contribution is made, you have an excellent candidate for elimination. For instance, you may be reviewing reports sent to you concerning activities in another department, information that you used to need but no longer have any use for. Or you may find yourself attending meetings that are no longer relevant to your work—a waste not only of your time but the committee's as well. If an activity does support some valued goal, is it worth the amount of time and energy you spend on it?

What Is the Agreement that Makes It Necessary for Me to Do This Activity?

For each activity you do, there is an agreement that it should be done. Agreements can be explicit or implicit, visible or invisible, conscious or unconscious. Next time you find yourself performing a task you are not sure you should do, ask yourself, "What is the invisible or unspoken agreement that says it is okay for me to do this activity? If it is a unilateral understanding, then should I stop doing it? If it is a bi-lateral or multilateral understanding, should I move to terminate the agreement and eliminate the task?" Do you have, for example, an invisible agreement with your boss and co-workers about what meetings you attend and what reports you will routinely and mechanically write up? Do you have an agreement with your children about your role as private chauffeur, house-keeper, and endless supplier of money?

If I Were to Stop Doing This Low-Payoff Activity, What Would Happen?

What would happen if you stopped making the beds at home for your teenage sons? What would happen if you stopped sending copies of the minutes to all regional managers? What would happen if you didn't fill out the endless forms you receive from some government agency? Who would miss it? What would be the worst that would happen? Stop doing a suspected unnecessary low-payoff task and see what happens.

The task of separating the necessary from the unnecessary is not always easy nor clear. Many times unnecessary tasks carry with them a high *presumption of legitimacy,* having once been legitimate uses of your time. Activities get done all the time that are presumed to be legitimate—papers that could be dumped into the wastebasket without any losses are filed away in burgeoning files, reports that aren't necessary are read.

Challenge the presumed legitimacy of activities by asking the question "What would happen if I didn't...?"

---

20 I have difficulty differentiating high and low payoffs.

Before you can differentiate your high payoffs (HIPOs) from your low payoffs (LOPOs), you must know what your valued goals are. In some cases, you will be working toward your own valued goal and in others, the management team's or the organization's. In your personal life, you may be working toward your youngster's (many parents discover that their valued goals are not necessarily the valued goals of their children), your family's, or your church's goal. In any case, before you can differentiate what activity makes a contribution to any goal, you must know the goal.

Our minds create countless excuses for spending time on LOPOs disguised as HIPOs. And it is easy to justify doing a LOPO because it *is* required or necessary. We must spend some time on LOPOs and sometimes most of the day is at the LOPO level, perhaps necessarily so. So it is important to be clear which activities actually make the difference in actualizing your goals; what are the activities that contribute substantially and significantly to your valued goals?

One manager remarked, "My whole job is one big LOPO." Another manager believes that everything he does in his work is a HIPO; that getting to work is a HIPO because he needs to be there to get the job done, that all the paperwork he does is a

HIPO because if it doesn't get done there will be trouble, and so on. But, of course, if everything you do is a HIPO, then nothing you do is a HIPO because no activity is valued more than any other.

---

21 I am not really sure how to set priorities. Are there any guidelines?

No task gets done until you give time to it and make it a priority to do. One definition of priority is "something requiring attention prior to competing alternatives"; another is "the preferential rating prescribing the order in which things are to be done." To give a task priority is to make a decision to do it prior to doing something else. Priorities have to do with time and doing—not wishing, hoping, or fantasizing, but doing. Your own priorities can be determined from the order in which you do things; that is, what you are actually doing is what you are giving priority to.

Here are some recommendations to help you clarify your priorities:

Know what your valued goals are   Thus you can evaluate the priorities placed on those activities that relate to these goals.

Remind yourself that a high-payoff activity does not necessarily receive a high priority   Some of the potentially highest-payoff activities are given low priority or, in some cases, no priority at all. It may be a high payoff for you to outline your best thinking about a new project and present it to management, but until it receives a high priority, it won't get done.

Recognize that no job is accomplished until it receives a high priority An activity becomes a high priority when time is given to it, and not before. It may be a high priority in your mind and your dreams, but it is not in reality until time is given to it.

Recognize that you fail to place a high priority on a high-payoff activity by allowing it to be postponed Either you place a high priority on a high-payoff activity or you don't. And until you do, the chances of accomplishing the task are nearly zero. An executive continually talks about what a high payoff it would be for him to start his own company, to do things the way he really wants to do them. But this is so much dream talk until he makes it a high enough priority to actually do it. So, while potentially a high payoff, starting his own business never gets done because it receives a low priority.

Make an effort to analyze and determine what your day's priorities should be at least once during the day This will give you a clear picture of what you are attempting to accomplish. One manager found it was best for him to take a spot check of his priorities for the day the first thing in the morning and again just after lunch. Stop for a moment during the day and simply ask yourself, "What am I attempting to accomplish today? What priority should I give these various activities?"

Take personal responsibility for your time and priorities, and acknowledge that you have chosen how you use your time Others can place time demands on you and influence your priorities, but within every demand and circumstance there is a part whether three percent or fifty percent that you can control.

When you are unclear about what your priorities should be, stop for a moment and ask yourself, "What is this day for?" What is its goal? What are the activities that are most important to accomplishing this goal for today? Some activities deserve high priority; some deserve no priority. Go back and check out the goals and the name of the game you happen to be playing at this time.

When you are unclear what your associates' priorities are, check with them to make sure that your understandings coincide What you think is a priority for your boss may not be one at all. The same principle holds true for your subordinates, co-workers, family, or friends.

Have faith in your judgment of your priorities and work to maintain them and reevaluate them at appropriate times No one is in a better position to know what your real values and priorities are than you.

Communicate your priorities to those who need to know them Letting others know makes your life and work better for you and for them. Few of us are mindreaders or walk on water regularly; few others, if any, seriously wonder what *our* priorities might be. We have all heard people say, "Well, he or she should have known that was a high priority for me." When asked how he or she "should have known," the answer often is ambiguous and self-centered. "Well, he is my boss," or, "I live with her. She should have known," or, "If he really cared he would have known." The best way to know, of course, is to communicate.

There is only one person fully, 100 percent, responsible for making sure that your priorities are understood and acted upon, and that person is you.

22   There are times during the week when I get hit with dozens of high priorities and have no way to get them all done. What can I do?

Unless you are superhuman, you can do only as much as your limitations and time allow. So when work is flying at you from every direction, use a high-priority reduction technique to control your workload. That is, do enough of each activity to move it out of the high-priority category and give you some breathing space. Then, return to the tasks later and complete them.

If, for example, you are confronted at the same time with four or five high-priority items, such as

- completing the quarterly financial report and sending it to the purchasing department,
- making conference arrangements for the middle-management workshop,
- drawing up a new marketing proposal, and
- making travel arrangements for the boss and confirming his appointments,

then do whatever you can now to reduce the urgency of each task.

For example:

1 Call purchasing and give them estimated figures, and send the completed report within the week.

2 Reserve the meeting room for the workshop and leave the details of table arrangements, food, and sound system until later.

3   Mail an outline of the marketing report together with a
    deadline for the completed job.
4   Call the airline. Confirm appointments the day before the
    trip.

The key is to keep from doing a sloppy job and to avoid
stop and start activity. Reduce the urgency, and then come
back to the task and give it your full attention when you are
under less pressure.

Of course, if you are continually under the gun with an
unrealistic number of priorities, it is time to clear this up with
yourself and your scorekeepers. Who is dumping these impossible priorities on you? What is keeping them there? How do
you feel about them?

If you have several bosses and/or subordinates with many
changing priorities, try this technique that one executive uses
successfully: she lets each petitioner believe that she is going to
handle his priority first. Then she selects the priority that she
feels is the most important and moves the others out of the
high-priority category as much as possible.

When it is humanly impossible to get all tasks done and
there's no one to whom you can delegate them, you must let
your scorekeepers know and then renegotiate your agreements. Or call a conference of all your scorekeepers, and let
them take responsibility for putting their priorities into an
order that they can live with and that you can handle.

One secretary uses a backwards calendar. Anyone bringing
in a rush job gets to pick a date on her calendar that promises
the work done before they gave it to her. So, if they bring it on
April 10 and need it "yesterday," they can have in on the ninth,
at least on her calendar. A humorous approach is often the best
tactic when inconsiderate or impossible demands are made of
you.

23   How can I best move to get an important but continually deferred task acted on?

After you have identified a deferred task that would be of advantage to do, consider the following suggestions for getting it done:

Set up immediate and valuable rewards for doing this activity
Regardless of what the deferred HIPO (high-payoff activity) is, immediately reward yourself when you spend time on it. Take yourself out on the town, buy yourself that ring you want, or take the afternoon off.

Remove false rewards for doing the low-payoff (LOPO) activities that drain time and are unnecessary and unproductive
Eliminate repetitive tasks, consolidate your correspondence, and reduce time spent on marginal reading. Realize that a false sense of busyness, comfortableness, and feeling in control of your time is a frequent reward of LOPOs and is counterproductive. Especially when compared to the rewards you receive from spending time on the HIPOs.

Divide and conquer   Take the HIPO and divide it into time-manageable parts. One busy executive said, "A high payoff for me is to reorganize a major project that has been needed desperately for the last several months, one that isn't getting done and probably will not be completed until I make it urgent to do. The way I approach this is to devote three quarters of an hour a day to the project, taking little time away from other important work."

Break the valued goal down into measurable goals   One way
to make the deferred HIPOs more manageable is to break
down the long-term goal into several short-term goals against
which progress can be measured more easily.

If your goal is to earn your graduate business degree, what
are the subgoals you must reach in order to accomplish this?
Do you need to prepare yourself to pass the graduate entrance
exams, to acquire a reading skill in a foreign language, or to
earn enough money to support yourself through graduate
school? Whatever the subgoals are, they will be more immediately manageable than the overall goal, and their accomplishment can provide you immediate satisfying reinforcement.

Identify the barriers to activating your deferred HIPOs
There may be several factors that are preventing you from
doing a deferred high-payoff activity. When you become aware
of them, you then can choose what you will do about them.
Barriers come in many shapes and sizes. Examples are:
ignorance of the alternatives available to you, lack of awareness that you can accomplish your HIPO activity in innovative
ways, or failure to realize that you can eliminate certain time-
consuming tasks. Other common barriers relate to the assumptions about what you are "supposed" to do and how you should
go about it.

Challenge your "have to's."   Make a list of the "have to's" that
are sapping your time, such as correspondence, telephone
inquiries, travel time, conference time, meeting time, report
reviewing, and writing. How many of these activities can be
eliminated? Do you have to attend all those meetings? Who
said so, and what is the implication if you don't? How much of
the correspondence really needs to be done by you? How much
is done out of habit? You will always "have to" do more than
you can do, and most of the "have to's" have little or nothing to
do with your purpose in life or the real essence of your work.

How many can you either eliminate, delegate, delay or do less completely to reduce the time and energy invested in them?

Block out HIPO time   Set aside special time for doing a certain deferred HIPO. Perhaps it's twenty-five minutes between the time you arrive at the office and your first appointment, or some other convenient time. One manager found that a high-payoff time for him to reflect and think creatively was directly after lunch. He walked to a nearby park, sat in the shade of a tree, and found that the forty minutes he invested three times a week were not only productive for his corporate work, but also refreshing, revitalizing, and downright enjoyable.

Another manager, instead of taking his lunch at the customary noon hour, goes to lunch at 1:00 P.M., misses much of the normal lunch traffic, and has a relatively uninterrupted time while the rest of the office is out to lunch.

Other executives make appointments with themselves. They simply have their secretaries block out an hour and a half on the calendar, just as they would with any appointment, and then they keep that appointment with themselves. Also, with flexible work scheduling becoming more popular, more managers are now able to arrange their schedules to work at home one or two mornings a week. This could be valuable time to reflect on some potential activity.

Have a HIPO place   Work on potentially high-payoff activities takes place in time and space, and some spaces are better for high-payoff work than others. Establish your own HIPO place. It could be a special park in your community, a particular room in your house, or a special part of your office. The important thing is that you view it as a HIPO place for you.

Align yourself with those who contribute to your reaching your goals Certain individuals are important to your well-being and contribute to your sense of accomplishment. Align with them and ask them to support you in placing a high priority on a deferred high payoff. Their encouragement may be just what you need to actualize it.

---

24   I need help in setting priorities and holding to them as agreed.

It is a challenge to set and maintain priorities that enhance and contribute to valued goals. The following suggestions are designed to help you with that challenge.

Communicate your priorities to your associates and those who are significant to you Ensure that friends, family, or co-workers understand what is important to you and why. Seek their help in managing your priorities.

Understand the priorities of others in your work and life relationships Find mutually beneficial ways to support each other's goals.

Discuss and obtain agreement with your boss on the priorities of your work responsibilities Both you and your manager need to be aware of the ground rules of the "game" you are playing as employee.

Be aware of your priority time limitations Just as you would not exceed a budget and run yourself into bankruptcy, do not exceed your time budget or you will end up time bankrupt, with no place to go to borrow more time.

Be increasingly aware of the rewards and penalties for doing and not doing certain activities   Some priorities carry higher penalties for not doing them than others. The failure to prepare yourself for a certain opportunity may not be apparent to you until too late. The penalties for continually postponing serious planning may show up too late for you to make the proper adjustment.

Make conscious decisions   Do not simply react to this time pressure or that time pressure. Ask yourself how each task supports a valued goal. What are the opportunities lost and what are the opportunities gained by assigning time to this activity and not to some other potential task? Everything you do has a cost, if only in terms of the time spent doing it. For example, when you drive to the grocery store, the cost is not only reflected in the food bill, but also in the time that you could have spent sleeping, watching the news, reading, relaxing, or golfing.

Consider all time valuable   Weigh your activities in terms of how time spent and effort expended contribute to valued goals, whether they be your own, others', your family's, your company's, or society's.

---

25   I need help understanding how my priorities are set on a daily basis. It seems like I work in a priority jungle.

Priority-setting is central to effective time management. Even if you don't know how priorities are actually being set, you probably have an idea how they ought to be set. Who has the authority and responsibility for setting them for you? For others? To whom are you accountable and how?

The two following suggestions will help clarify how your priorities are set on a daily basis in the office:

1 Do an inventory of all duties for which you are responsible, such as conducting staff meetings, completing certain reports, making client calls, or reviewing product and research proposals.

2 Conduct a personal time study for a few days to see what is actually happening with your time. This will give you some idea of the relationship between time and task performance.

Now, after completing these, write beside each task or responsibility whether it receives a high, medium, or low priority. Note also who determines that one activity is to receive priority attention over another. Is it your boss, an agreement with clients, a practice of the company, your decision, or a combination of these?

While it is probably not feasible to ascertain the exact priority of each task over another, try to get a general feeling. For instance, who requires the daily reports and do they take precedence over meeting with a client? Who requires you to read incoming mail, and when? Who says it is a priority for you to answer all telephone inquiries; would this be better handled by a receptionist, an answering service, your secretary, or a central exchange?

Often there is little correlation between the priority placed on an activity and its real payoff. Some of the highest-payoff activities are given low and sometimes no priority, while some of the lowest-payoff activities (such as reading the morning mail or talking with co-workers about last night's pro football game) receive a high priority.

Priorities are set in various ways, and while some make sense many are unproductive. Here are a few of the key ways they get set on a daily basis. Is it any wonder that sometimes we feel like we are working in a priority jungle?

Daily Pressures—Squeaky Wheels

Each day brings different and often conflicting time pressures from co-workers, supervisors, or clients, and these daily pressures often determine priorities on a hit and miss, haphazard, or first-come–first-served basis. What starts out to be a perfectly normal day ends up being a series of responses to that particular day's pressures.

So what gets done are the urgent tasks, not necessarily the important ones that make a vital contribution to your objectives. It may be urgent for you to handle a worker's grievance or to put out "brushfires," but it is seldom important. What is seen as urgent is to get this or that report completed and sent out before corporate headquarters cries for it, even if the report is rarely, if ever, read. Clients who seem to have nothing better to do than call and complain about some insignificant problem (of course it may not seem insignificant to them), secretaries who complain about how the lunch breaks are handled, someone who continually badgers you for this or that report—these are all examples of squeaky wheels.

Like babies who cry to get their bottles, squeaky wheels squeak until they are greased. Sometimes the squeaky wheel deserves the grease, but it almost always *gets* the grease: your attention, your time, and your energy.

Determine to what degree these daily pressures and squeaky wheels have legitimate demands on your time and how you best can manage them.

Personal Preference

Priorities are sometimes set simply according to what you want to do. Managers often find, however, that what they want to do first is not necessarily the best use of their time. Many choose to read the newspaper first thing in the morning under the guise of getting caught up with what's happening in the world. But unless you are a financial advisor and need to read the *Wall Street Journal* as part of your work, the value of newspaper reading is questionable. Even more abusive to the effective use of time is opening, reading, and then responding to the morning mail. This often is the first order of business because many individuals have a personal preference to see immediately what the mail carrier brought them—a little like Christmas every day. But, generally, opening mail can be left until later in the day, and your secretary can handle far more of your daily incoming mail than you may appreciate.

Check out your personal preferences in terms of how you set priorities. Are they supportive of the purpose of the day?

Prisoner of the Past

Many priorities are priorities because they have been that way for some time and have become customary or habitual. The attitude reflected is, "We've (I've) always done it this way." Are you locked into attending meetings, going to the grocery store, or handling a project on your own when it isn't a good use of your time anymore? Habit can be a real time saver in doing activities that take little or no thought, but habits can also chain you to behavior that is not productive and should be changed. Invalid priorities may hide behind tradition and custom.

Whatever Hits First

Too often things get done and priorities are set on a first noticed, first done basis. A telephone call comes in, you answer it. Someone drops by your office to chat, you chat. A magazine is placed in your basket, you read it.

Priorities Set by Others

Others—boss, co-workers, clients—may be setting priorities for you. Many are legitimate, but some probably aren't. You are accountable to your boss according to your agreements and job responsibilities; you may also be accountable in various ways to your organization, your family, and others for how you use parts of your time. You are accountable because you have agreed in some way to be accountable within the role you have chosen to play—the role of employee, parent, friend, or member of your community.

Check to see what your agreements, your unspoken understandings, are regarding priorities set by others. Which activities in your job take priority over others? How do others' priorities for you fit into your own priority scheme? How do you resolve conflict if there is a discrepancy between what you and another think should be a priority for you? Often your priorities are set by others because you have not been clear with them about what your own priorities are. When your boss, co-workers, friends, and spouse are not clear about what you consider a priority, they may believe it absolutely appropriate to set your priorities for you.

Once you have a clear idea of how your priorities are being set and how your time gets committed, you can decide how you want to manage your situation. Some priorities you may want to renegotiate with others and some you may want to upgrade, while you may decide to give a lower priority or no priority to others. It may help your thinking to group your activities according to common characteristics, such as the following:

Time the task takes Some priorities, such as okaying a request or signing a document, should be handled immediately because they can be done quickly and may keep you from holding others up. You get the task out of the way in a minimum amount of time and gain momentum to move on other more important and time-consuming tasks.

Timing of the task Certain activities deserve immediate priority simply because it is more efficient to do them immediately than let them go and then have to come back to them cold. If you are responsible for the meeting minutes, for example, write down the essential information you need before leaving the meeting room. Then hand it to the typist to be prepared. Doing this immediately saves you from fretting about the task and prevents your having to face a cold, if not unattractive, set of notes later.

Frequency of the task Some individual tasks are best handled by not doing them until they can be bunched together and then given priority. Tasks like returning telephone calls, preparing routine correspondence, and collecting project data may advantageously be postponed until another time.

Importance of the task When a task is important but can be easily postponed, make special note of the task's importance and then place a high priority on getting it done. All too often important and high-payoff activities are deferred during the rush and pressures of the day. High-payoff, important tasks, deserve high priority—choose to place that priority on those tasks. They will seldom, if ever, be urgent to do. You will need to take the initiative to make those HIPOs (be they strategic planning, clearing up a serious but important misunderstanding, or establishing objectives and goals) urgent to do.

Amount of control you have over the priority Categorize tasks according to the amount of priority control you have over them. When you are the one who determines a task's priority, you can choose to do it earlier in the morning or later in the day. This will allow you to put some flexibility into your daily schedule.

How it affects others   If a task can be done in a relatively short time and if your doing it will free someone else to get his or her job done, it may need immediate attention. Forcing others to wait for your signature on a report, or for your data for a project, can unnecessarily aggravate them and impair your working and personal relationships with them.

The most effective way to manage your priority jungle is to be as clear as possible about what your goals are and make a strong commitment to reaching them. Priorities then have a strange and almost magical way of falling into place. Not that the daily pressures stop or time demands made by others evaporate—but your central purpose and intentions are then clear and you are able to make judgments and manage priorities in a more purposeful, targeted way.

Getting a Grip
On Time

Scales and clocks ar-re not to be thrusted to decide annything that's worth deciding. Who tells time be a clock? Ivry hour is th'same to a clock an' ivry hour is diff'rent to me. Wan long, wan short.

Finley Peter Dunne, *Mr. Dooley Says*, 1910

One of the first steps in organizing time is to find out where and how you are currently using time. Record what you do during the day and you will most likely be surprised to find out how your time is actually being used. Time that you think you are spending on planning or team-building often shows up quite differently in an accurate time review.

This chapter will give you concerted steps in organizing time: how to get a grip on time, how to get started more quickly on the day's assignments, how to avoid many of the constant interruptions of the day.

26 How can I organize my time at the office? I really need specifics.

The first step in organizing time is to determine what you and your organization want to accomplish, and then to keep those goals in mind. Know the purpose of your work, the agreements, time pressures, and constraints under which you are working. Listed below are some time-organizing techniques that support effective use of time. You can't accomplish what you want to unless you organize for it.

Strive to achieve balance   Consider which activities demand immediate attention and which are not urgent but have important payoffs tomorrow, next week, next month, or next year. It is easy in the day-to-day battle of the time game to lose track of the game's purpose.

Many managers remark that they are so busy doing daily tasks, working with subordinates, and handling complaints and paperwork that they find little or no time for long-range and high-payoff activities like planning, creative thinking, or reviewing. It is easy to fall into the trap of being so busy organizing time to meet daily needs (which are often only maintenance) that we fail to make time for more important but easily deferred activities. Strive for balance.

Organize your day so that you have flexible time available for emergencies or opportunities that may come up unexpectedly As you know, they will come up. Some managers like to leave an hour or two in the early afternoon as a cushion against the unexpected. Some have tentatively scheduled activities that are purposely scheduled with flexibility in case a higher priority comes up. These scheduled activities can then be shifted around, leaving time for the unexpected.

Determine approximately how much time a project will take and then add a little more Allow for unanticipated intrusions, problems, or miscalculations.

Organize the day for maximum efficiency Some tasks are more efficiently performed at certain times of the day. For example, the morning hours typically are high-energy periods, times to count on your alertness and to use to the fullest advantage. Using this time to read your mail is probably a mistake, especially when there is usually nothing in it that can't wait until later.

Also take into consideration the schedules and needs of others. If it is easier to get everyone together in the hours just before closing time, arrange the meeting for then; if the best time to return phone calls and contact clients is the hour before noon, organize your schedule accordingly.

Organize time around activities that make high payoffs to your personal goals or the organization's High-payoff (HIPO) activities—particularly the ones that are not urgent to do—need to have time intentionally and persistently allocated to them or they will not get done. The low payoffs (LOPOs)—routine paperwork, meetings, complaints, and problems—will tend to dominate unless you guard against them.

Organize time around priorities Make time for high-payoff activities by making them time-critical to do. Unless you organize your day to do so, it is probable that only the low payoffs will get time, while the potential HIPOs languish, time-starved. Ask yourself, "Is this a high-priority task for me to do? If so, why, and who says so, and how do I feel about it?" When you get into the habit of seeing your day as a series of tasks and responsibilities with relative priorities, you have opened the door to using your time purposefully and effectively.

Determine the right investment of time Make efforts to determine what the right investment of time is for a task, both in terms of quality and quantity. What is the right investment of time for me for working on a one-to-one basis with my staff? What is the right investment of time for specialized planning, for going through routine paperwork, for attending meetings, for public relations? Get into the habit of asking this question: What is the right investment of time for this activity, now and in the future?

Seek the cooperation of others for your time commitments Let them know how you would like to spend your time—today, tomorrow, this week, and in general. Let them know (when appropriate) what your priorities are and what your purpose is

today, next week. Understand what their priorities are, what
they would like to accomplish, and how they would like to
spend their time.

In summary, there is no one right way to organize your
time. What works for one may not be proper for another. Your
goals will, in part, determine how time needs to be organized,
what the agreements, priorities, and requirements are, and how
they impact on time organization. Organizing tools, which are
discussed elsewhere in this section, will help to support you
after some basic decisions are made about what you want to
accomplish.

---

27   How can I get a better grip on where my time goes?

It is important to know where time goes in order to successfully
manage it, and a simple time study will give you that
information. The simpler the time study the better. An
elaborate, complicated study is neither necessary nor helpful
and will tend to waste more time than it saves. One time
inventory required managers to log their activities at ten-
minute intervals. They were so preoccupied with filling in the
blanks that they accomplished nothing else, and the study gave
a distorted picture of the day. Moreover, everyone resented the
system so much that they sabotaged it by misrepresenting the
way they really used time during the day.

So, make it simple and honest. An effective tool for
recording your daily activities is the personal time study
worksheet (Figure 1). Simply jot down what took place, how
long it took, and any comments you have. Strictly record the

Personal Time Study Worksheet

NAME _____

DATE _____

Morning			Afternoon		
	What Took Place?	Time Duration	Comments	What Took Place?	Time Duration	Comments

Reflections on the day:

Figure 1 Personal time study worksheet.

facts. Avoid judgmental statements like "another hour down the drain" or "this is Helen's job." Do, however, note the origin of the task—whether it is required by your boss, required by the system, or is the result of your own initiative.

You will, of course, lie. That is, you will write "meeting with Philip for team-building" when in truth you had a bull session; you may write "creative planning time" instead of "day-dreaming and worrying." There is nothing wrong with such lies, as long as you know you are stretching the truth. The last person in the world who should believe them is you.

You may want to keep the results of the study confidential at first, since they can be disappointing and threatening. When you review your own record and find out you've been goofing off, concentrating on low-payoff tasks, failing to delegate, and generally managing your time ineffectively, it can be a shock.

But after you have recorded your daily activities for a few days, you should be ready to evaluate them. You may want to invite your secretary, colleagues, or boss to help. Or if you are conducting a leisure-time study, consider sharing these data with some of your significant others (spouse, children, parents, friends).

1   What am I now doing that I don't have to do and actually doesn't need to be done by anyone? (Eliminate any unnecessary activity.)

2   What am I now doing that I don't have to do but needs to be done by someone? (Delegate it.)

3   What am I now doing that I have to do but can be done in a different way to save time? (Streamline it.)

4   What am I now doing that wastes my time?

5   What am I now doing that wastes others' time?

6   What am I now doing that must continue to be done just this way?

7 What am I now doing that is really worthwhile doing?

8 What am I not doing that I ought to be spending time on?

9 What am I not doing that really doesn't need to be done? (Stop feeling guilty.)

10 Have I been completely honest with myself about these tasks?

11 What does this data say to me about the way I manage my time? What do ceaseless telephone calls, interruptions, uncertain priorities, and jammed calendars say about me?

12 Which activities are the most rewarding?

13 Which activities are the least rewarding?

14 Which activities are the most threatening to me?

Review the time study again for more precise information and consider the following questions and suggestions.

- Is the time between activities—between appointments or phone calls—used well?

- Is there dead time (for example, canceled appointments) that might be used more productively?

- How much time is spent starting up or winding down? Do you need to "get into the mood" for certain tasks or to take a breather after others? If you're interrupted, do you have to start again from scratch?

- What activities might be properly batched together to reduce start-up and wind-down time and reduce interruptions? Some good batching candidates include telephone calls, correspondence, errands, and report writing.

- Identify how priorities were established for the tasks you completed. Were priorities planned or was the order of the tasks a response to crises, accidental, demanded by others,

decided by your secretary, or determined by whatever was
on top of the other junk on your desk?

• Look at the relationship between each task and its
  contribution to valued goals. Are the easiest, least important tasks always the first to get done? Do the most
  important activities have to wait?

• What do you intend to do, now that you've completed the
  time study? Anything? When and how? Whose support do
  you need? Who will be affected by your efforts?

The time-design charts (Figures 2 and 3) are supplements to
the personal time study worksheet and can give you additional
valuable help in seeing where your time goes.

Many executives and managers use brief, periodic time
reviews to keep themselves on target. Once a month is usually
often enough to shock one back into a more purposeful time-
conservation effort.

A simple time study will give you a picture of how your time
is being spent. Often what the study does is to point out that too
much of your time is invested in too many low-payoff activities
that would be better either eliminated or delegated. The study
may show you that the timing of certain activities would be
enhanced if placed earlier or later in the day.

It is really impossible to manage your time effectively until
you first have an accurate picture of what happens to it. A good
time study will give you this information. But be prepared for
some real surprises: how you think you are using your time and
how you really are using your time may be two quite different
realities.

TODAY'S TIME DESIGN

Name _____ Date _____

Todays Schedule

6:30 _____	1:00 _____
7:00 _____	1:30 _____
7:30 _____	2:00 _____
8:00 _____	2:30 _____
8:30 _____	3:00 _____
9:00 _____	3:30 _____
9:30 _____	4:00 _____
10:00 _____	4:30 _____
10:30 _____	5:00 _____
11:00 _____	5:30 _____
11:30 _____	6:00 _____
12:00 _____	6:30 _____
12:30 _____	7:00 _____

Action Items Today	Priority Hi/Med/Low	Estimate Time	Estimate Hour To Do	What Actually Happened	Comments
1.					
2.					
3.					
4.					
5.					
6.					
7.					

Phone Calls (see phone book for record of calls)

1. _____	6. _____
2. _____	7. _____
3. _____	8. _____
4. _____	9. _____
5. _____	10. _____

Appointments, Meetings

With Whom	Purpose	Action Required	Comments
1.			
2.			
3.			
4.			

Items Promised To Others

1. _____
2. _____
3. _____
4. _____

Things To Be Sent To Me

1. _____
2. _____
3. _____
4. _____

Projects In Progress To Work On

1. _____
2. _____
3. _____
4. _____

Miscellaneous

©Rutherford Training Workshops Inc., 1979. Note: This form does not work— unless you make it work.

Figure 2   Today's time design.

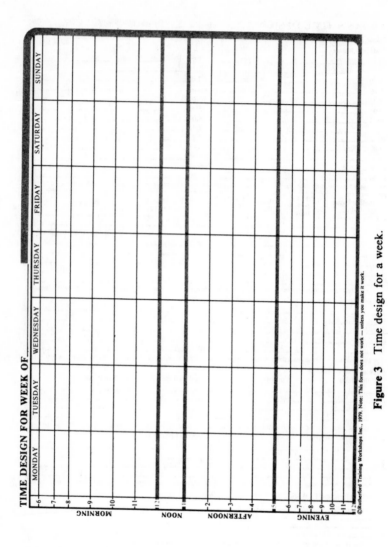

Figure 3   Time design for a week.

28   I am continually interrupted and have to stop and start what I am doing. How can I avoid this?

We live in a world of continuous interruptions. Formal studies of how managers use their time have revealed that they typically have no more than seven to twenty minutes of continuous time before being interrupted by a phone call, a meeting, or a visitor. Starting and stopping work for many is a way of life. Have you ever arrived at the office with every intention of working for two straight hours on an important report? Then, all of the sudden, the phones start ringing, visitors drop in, staff members ask for your help, and your boss calls an emergency meeting. Your planned two hours of work become instead three or four hours—of interruptions.

Any attempt to organize your time must have a degree of flexibility built in. "Flexibility" does not mean, though, that you must give up any serious attempt to control the starts and stops you face daily at work and at home.

One of the most significant miscalculations managers and professionals make is misjudging the time necessary to obtain desired results. When too much or too little time is allotted to accomplish a task satisfactorily, time is being wasted. Review your work activities and note that they require different amounts of time.

Some activities lend themselves to small time blocks. Others—often the more important, high-payoff activities, such as employee or product development—take larger blocks of time. To spend less than the necessary amount of time is a waste. If a project takes four continuous hours to complete, spending thirty minutes here and thirty minutes there may not only be a waste of time but a source of frustration, resentment, and hopelessness that interferes with other duties.

When...	*Then...*
You feel your day is being chopped up and you don't know where your time goes,	Conduct a selective time study. Monitor your interruptions and collect data on where your time goes.
You want a more continuous block of time and are having trouble finding it,	Work to block out one or two hours of continuous time by batching related activities. For example, make phone calls at the same time when possible and do correspondence once or twice a day only, not every time you think of a letter that should go out.
The stop-start activity is a result of interruptions by others,	Seek their assistance in avoiding the stop-start syndrome. Renegotiate agreements, if necessary. Be honest with them about your time needs, in a way that doesn't make them feel guilty for what they have done.
The stop-start activity is a result of your own interruptions,	Apply the "first things first" strategy of determining what is the best activity to work on *now*. Set specific time limits and stick to them. Create a supportive personal environment by keeping your desk clear of irrelevant material—eliminate visible distractors and put away more interesting reading material not pertinent to that day's work.

When...	*Then...*
You are not clear about how much time certain activities will take,	Estimate how much time you will give to each activity and chart time allocations for the day. Review at the end of the day what was accomplished when compared to the day's plan. Reward yourself in some significant way when you have concentrated on planned tasks.
You stop doing something,	Make a note of where you are on the project. Take a few seconds and note any pertinent remarks about what you are thinking and where you want to start immediately when you get back to it.

29   How can I find uninterrupted time to plan, think, and create? I often need at least two hours of such time for special work.

Interruptions and time pressures easily become a way of life, certainly at work but also in nonwork activities. Outlined here are methods of arranging time within the working day (or during off-work hours) to give you some quiet, uninterrupted time.

Establish time norms   Estimate how much time you need to complete a task successfully. Do you need one hour of quiet time a day or one hour a week? For example, how much time should you devote to a subordinate's performance review? What is the normal amount of time you should spend reviewing computer reports from the marketing division?

Block appropriate amounts of time   Some tasks require a certain amount of time, and spending less than that amount may actually waste time. If you need two hours to finish a project and spend only thirty-five minutes on it, that thirty-five minutes may not just be lost—it actually may hurt the project by increasing frustration, giving a sense of hopelessness, or suggesting that enough time has been spent when it hasn't.

Make an appointment with yourself   Make a formal appointment with yourself and respect it as you would an appointment with an important client, your boss, or a co-worker. It is worthy of your respect, for a serious appointment with yourself can be more important than others on your calendar.

If someone calls or drops by to see you during your "appointment," your secretary can (with a totally clear conscience) say, "I am sorry, my manager is in an important conference right now." It might be thought-provoking to say to the caller, "I am sorry, my manager is not available—she has an important appointment with herself," but that is not recommended.

Be flexible, as you would be with any other important appointment. If your most important client calls and wants to place a $5,000,000 order immediately, I think the best course of action would be to cancel the appointment with yourself. Before you cancel it, however, set a firm alternative date. Don't let it slip—a meeting with yourself is easily put off.

Batch shorter items together Some tasks fit easily and logically together—certain correspondence, telephone calls, appointments, or meetings—and can be grouped together in order to free blocks of uninterrupted time. You are not really creating any *more* time; you are simply rearranging the distribution of your time. This technique can reduce the "stop-start syndrome"—having to stop to handle an interruption and then spend extra start time to get going again when you come back to the task.

Rearrange the day When you want three of four continuous hours of uninterrupted time, try scheduling the work session from 10:00 to 3:00, taking a late breakfast and late lunch. Or schedule the work session from 3:30 to 7:30 and have a late dinner. You need not be locked into the traditional 9:00 to 12:00, 1:00 to 5:00 schedule with all its possibilities for interruptions. Of course, you might want to start even earlier to get a couple of hours head start on the normal day.

One management group found that they got the most done when they began planning and briefing meetings at 4:00 P.M. and ran through until 8:30 P.M., after which they went to dinner together. This schedule allowed them to handle a full day and still get in four and a half hours of uninterrupted work. This worked far better for them than for all eight people attempting to get together during regular working hours.

Let others know when is the best time to contact you The simple policy of letting others know when they can best contact you can reduce many unnecessary or untimely calls. At the same time, let your clients, co-workers, and others know when is *not* a good time to contact you, such as during time you have blocked out for special projects. They will appreciate this courtesy and it will support you both: they will not waste their time trying to contact you when you are not available, and you will save your time by eliminating "while you were out" phone messages.

30 How can I get started more quickly in the morning?

Nothing will get you started before you have decided to get started, but there are some techniques to support you once you have made that decicion.

Follow a specific, automatic routine first thing in the morning
Some executives work out in a gym or jog to get the day started. They don't think about it, they don't try to get started, they just do it automatically. If they thought about getting up out of a warm bed at six in the morning to pump iron or run a couple of miles, they'd probably never do it.

Before you go to sleep, visualize exactly what you are going to do when you get up   Experience getting started on it and imagine doing it. Note how it feels, revel in the power you gain over your day, and enjoy the rewards that come to you.

Establish a place to get started   Define the spot where the action begins and the act that begins it. It might be sitting at your desk reviewing the day with your secretary, reading the financial page on the commuter train, or dictating letters in your car. Wherever it is, your arrival there signals the beginning of your day.

Set a definite time to get started   When you arrive at the office, get to work immediately instead of lingering over coffee or reading the newspaper. Or begin work with a prompt, daily staff meeting to clarify the day's priorities and maintain communication.

Make whatever you get started on worth while   It doesn't have to be the most important or most difficult or most pressing activity you have scheduled for the day, but it should be useful, like calling the answering service or setting up appointments.

Note exactly where you leave off work every day   You will then need a minimum of start-up time to get going again the next morning, eliminating frustration and reorientation time.

Set up a reward and punishment system   When you get started without much lag time, reward yourself with a ten-minute break. Similarly, if you don't get started as you feel you should, penalize yourself by passing up a scheduled break or lunch with your friends. Get in the habit of rewarding and penalizing yourself as a support technique.

Carpe diem ("seize the day")   Get up and capture the day before it flies away. Take advantage of all the time you have—don't squander it. Start with a good beginning and the rest of the day will take care of itself.

---

31   How can I make better use of my air-travel time?

In-flight time is often perfect for business and personal correspondence that gets put off at the office. Ask your secretary to prepare a packet of stationery, carbon paper, and stamped, addressed envelopes. You can get at least ten brief letters out of the way during a two-hour flight and still listen to music, eat, and take a cat nap. You may even receive compliments on your personal touch in this world of computerized letters. Drop the letters in the airport mailbox when your reach your destination. A carbon of such notes is useful for future reference, but carbon or not, personal correspondence gets the message out fast, frees your secretary for other work, saves dictation time, and humanizes your business.

In-flight time also provides a good opportunity to get caught up on your reading, whether trade journals, news magazines, or just a good book. You won't be interrupted by drop-ins, phone calls, or a single office crisis.

Travel time is also useful for getting your thoughts and plans down on tape. Many executives take a dictaphone machine on trips to record the results of business meetings, names and addresses of new contacts, and other information they want on file.

Use a travel agent when possible. Travel agents can save time and sometimes money and there is no charge to you. Some typical services include making rental-car reservations, booking hotel and motel accommodations, and getting theater tickets. Travel agents often have inside information that will make your trip more pleasant. Also, ask the agent for time-saving flights.

Most airlines have flight clubs that you can join. They are semiprivate, peaceful havens away from the crowds and noise of the terminal, which provide services such as complimentary cocktails and soft drinks, telephones, conference rooms, and other comforts and time savers. The modest club fee is quickly made up in convenience and soothed nerves.

Carry on your suitcase and hand luggage, and you won't have to wait in the baggage-claim line. Keeping your bags with you also avoids lost or delayed luggage problems. If you can't carry them on with you, at least take everything you need to conduct business. Also, put I.D. tags inside as well as outside your baggage in case it gets lost or your name is torn off or obliterated. Being prepared for emergencies is absolutely essential for the jet-age executive.

You can also subscribe to *Pocket Flight Guide,* an inexpensive, official monthly airline publication that can save time, frustration, and possibly your neck. One executive arrived at the Denver airport in early evening to catch a flight to St. Louis, only to be told it had been canceled and that no other flights were scheduled for that day. But in his guide, he discovered that the harried clerk had overlooked a plane with another airline leaving in fifteen minutes. Moving quickly, he was able to make the flight and meet his business commitments. This one incident definitely paid for many months' subscription.

32 Unfinished tasks seem to interfere with my other work. What can I do to eliminate this problem?

Cultivate a killer instinct where unfinished business is concerned: refuse to let it dominate you. Unfinished business is a double time waster. Not only does it nag at you, interfering with other work, but it requires warm-up time to get back into.

Encourage yourself to complete tasks by:

1 Committing yourself to completing a job and rewarding yourself immediately when it's done. Take five minutes to relax, go for a walk, or do something else you want to do.
2 Imagining how it will feel when the job is finished. Anticipate the relief and the sense of control you will enjoy.

3 Imagining how it would feel not to finish the job. Anticipate the penalties and negative results of not completing the task.

These techniques can be applied to big tasks as well as to small ones. An annual report, project recommendation, or similar assignment can be subdivided and approached as a series of smaller, more manageable units. With the completion of each step you will experience increasing control over the total task.

Relationships, both personal and professional, can also be dominated by unfinished business. In fact, it can ruin a perfectly good connection with a friend or colleague. If you don't tell your boss how you feel when he wastes your time or you hesitate to ask a friend to stop doing something that bothers you, your energy is diverted into anger, resentment, anxiety, frustration, insecurity, self-pity, or any of a dozen other bad feelings. Acknowledge that you have an unexpressed feeling—some unfinished business. Use the killer instinct to get it off your chest and clear the air. You will save time and energy and will unquestionably enhance your sense of well-being and control.

---

33   What shall I do with spare moments that come up during the day—waiting for someone to pick me up, waiting for a return phone call?

Spare moments, like waiting time, are usually five minutes here and fifteen minutes there. They are often wasted and experienced as boring, frustrating, and unproductive. But you can turn these moments to your advantage and, instead of pacing the floor or thumbing through an outdated magazine, use this time to do any number of things.

- Bring your daily record book up to date.
- Update your expense account.
- Make a shopping list.
- Plan a meeting, party, or strategy.
- Think of better ways to manage your time, at the office and at home.
- Observe what is happening around you. Notice the decor of the room, the expression on people's faces, the texture of the wall paint, thereby increasing your observation power.
- Write down three short tasks you would like to accomplish that day. Choose things that take less than ten minutes to do and do one on the spot.
- Write yourself a note about something important, such as the way you feel about your work, personal life, spouse, or teenage son.
- Identify a situation in which you want to say no and prepare a script to deal with it.
- Determine what you will accomplish during the next ten minutes of filler time that becomes available to you.
- Write a letter. If you plan ahead, you'll be prepared with letterhead, carbon paper, and a stamped envelope. Make it brief, write clearly, and let your correspondent know he or she is important enough to receive a personal note.

View spare moments as gifts of time, rare opportunities to change pace. Then you will receive double value from these filler time minutes: you will avoid frustration and annoyance of waiting, and you will be able to convert this otherwise unproductive time into time to use as you choose.

---

34   It never fails—whenever I'm working against a deadline, I'm inundated with requests for my time.

It may seem that you get more of these calls when you are under pressure because you are more acutely aware of your time and the need to make the most of it. When you are not particularly concerned about how you are using your time, intrusions may even be welcome. Your hyperawareness makes you hyper-sensitive to demands on your time.

In order to manage this situation more effectively, there are several actions you might explore:

1   When you know you're going to be extremely busy before a deadline, clear your calendar. Provide ample blocks of scheduled, uninterrupted time.

2   Tell clients who might call you that this is a bad time of the year (week, month, day) to try to reach you. See if you can cut off their requests at the pass by answering or anticipating questions before they arise.

3   Set up a special hot-line hour during which you will be available.

4   Figure out how many hours you need to complete your project and allot half again as much.

5   Isolate yourself—make your whereabouts known only to your partner or assistant. Use a colleague's office for the two or three hours of uninterrupted time you need.

35 How do I avoid taking work home with me that should be done at the office?

If you are regularly and continually taking work home with you that should have been done at the office, you are a victim of negative time expansion: time expanding to accommodate the work allotted to it.

During any eight hours of work time, a certain amount of work will be accomplished when time is effectively managed. Let X represent this amount. When time is not well managed you will get less than X completed. If you then allow the time allotted for X to expand to include 7:00 to 9:00 P.M., you fall victim to the law of negative time expansion. You have allowed what you could have done during the proper work hours to expand into your after-work hours.

This is a corollary of what is referred to as Parkinson's Law, which states that work tends to expand to accommodate the time allotted to it. (Example: If you have twenty-five minutes to clean your desk, then that is the time it takes; if you have an hour, it will take an hour.) Managers are less prone to fall victim to Parkinson's Law than many other workers because they usually have more to do than time to do it and therefore rarely have time on their hands to lose.

But often they allow work to expand into after-work hours, work that they could have completed during regular working hours if it were not for lack of concentration and failure to manage their time well.

(The idea of negative time expansion includes only those work activities that are more appropriately done at the office. It does not encompass work you deliberately decide to spend time on at home. Unlike the overflow work we have been talking about, work you choose to take home is not a result of unconsciously—or consciously—goofing off during the day at the office, of dallying, or of failing to set realistic deadlines. It is work you simply choose to do at home.)

Here is a case history of a victim of negative time expansion.

Bill J. found his briefcase full of papers, reports, and unfinished correspondence as he left the office at 5:45 after a hard day's work. He never seemed to get everything done during regular work hours. Bill's boss recently commented to Bill that he felt there was a problem if Bill needed to work an additional two to three hours several nights a week at home.

Bill was concerned, too. Together they agreed that Bill would make a simple, personal time study of what he did during the day. He would log his activities in approximatley half-hour intervals for five working days without making a big production of it, and then he would review the data.

On completion of the time study, Bill was shocked. Instead of showing a hard-driving, efficient manager, overworked but effectively meeting the challenges of the day, the study drew quite a different picture. He found he was wasting time in a stop-start syndrome, interrupting others, and being in turn interrupted by them needlessly and unproductively. Instead of planning and organizing his work, he was falling victim to lack of clear goals and poor personal organization. He took extended lunch breaks, involved himself in excessive socializing, and was lost in preoccupation and daydreaming that prevented him from concentrating on the important management tasks at hand.

The example of Bill J. is not extreme. When you find yourself in a situation of carrying work home night after night, you can do the following:

1 *List the activities you do at home that you think should more appropriately be done at the office.* Joslyn M., a

manager in a large corporation, was working two hours almost every night at home after work, and it was affecting her relationship with her family. She took pen and pad and noted the work that she was taking home with her that she should have been doing at the office, which included dictating correspondence to clients, reading reports from other departments on new products in production, and getting caught up on overdue reports. Next to each activity inappropriately done at home she indicated the amount of time it took.

2 *List the activities you did at work in place of the important activities you should have done there but did at home instead.* When Joslyn did this, her list looked something like this:

- Spent too much time simply chitchatting with co-managers.
- Didn't concentrate while reviewing important reports.
- Got up and down from my desk, went to the bathroom as an excuse for not doing my work, and fantasized about my relationships, real and imagined.
- Jumped from one task to another without finishing any of them.

3 *Compare the two inventories (of the activities you did inappropriately at home and the activities that you did at the office that you shouldn't have).* When Joslyn reviewed hers she was embarrassed, but she was also delighted to discover areas that she could immediately change in order to better use time.

4 *Select an important activity that you are inappropriately doing at home.* Joslyn selected getting caught up on overdue reports, which took about an hour of her evening time.

5 *Select an activity performed during working hours that actually wastes your time. Replace this time-wasting,*

undesired activity with the more important, desired task.
Joslyn selected the excessive time she was spending chitchatting and replaced it with catching up on her overdue
reports. She found she made significant headway in
gaining control over her time and the battle with negative
time expansion.

6   *Repeat the process with your two activity inventories until
you have recaptured your time at work or have made some
time decisions on what you really want to do with your
time.*

After completing a time and activity inventory, you may
find you don't want to change anything. You may like the idea
of being able to dally away a half-hour here and there at work
and prefer to "make up" this time after office hours. Fine, if
that is what you want to do with your time. Do it, however, as a
conscious choice.

Joslyn decided that her personal time and family time were
more important to her than what she gained from chitchat and
daydreaming on the job. She was able to retrain herself to pay
closer attention to getting her job done within the work day,
freeing her leisure time to spend in other pursuits.

If your negative time expansion is encouraged and sup-
ported by others, be honest with them. Let them know that you
are concerned about losing time at work and that it is affecting
the rest of your life. Ask for their assistance. If, as in the case of
Joslyn, there is excessive chitchat, share your concern with
your co-workers. Suggest, perhaps, that they limit their drop-
in visit to ten minutes instead of a half-hour, or that you limit
your social conversation primarily to break and lunch time. By
repossessing inappropriately used work time, you can get your
job done during the day and still have the camaraderie of your
co-workers. You may even want to make an alternative time
for your dallying and goofing off—maybe during commuting
or right after work.

Constantly guard against the negative affects of allowing time to drift and expand inappropriately, intruding on other valuable time.

---

36 I have constant interruptions throughout the day. How can I better understand why this is happening?

I would recommend that you make a Selective Interruption Time Study, which is designed to monitor your interruptions.

The most significant interruptions may not at first be obvious, for instance, the amount of time you interrupt yourself during the day. You are your own worst time waster when you are preoccupied, get up for a cup of coffee or a cigarette, shuffle paper around, go to the bathroom, make unnecessary phone calls, chat with your secretary, or search for something you've "misplaced."

Studies indicate that the average manager lives a continuously interrupted work life, subject to intrusions by phone, visitors, questions, meetings, and the like. On the average, he or she is interrupted every fifteen minutes. Does that fit your own experience? What's worse, if managers are not interrupted at least once each half hour, they interrupt themselves, say those same studies. If you're like other managers, you'll make a phone call or use your intercom or open the door of your office just to make sure the building hasn't been evacuated. You'll do something—anything—just to make contact with people.

Use the chart in this chapter as a way to zero in on your interruptions:

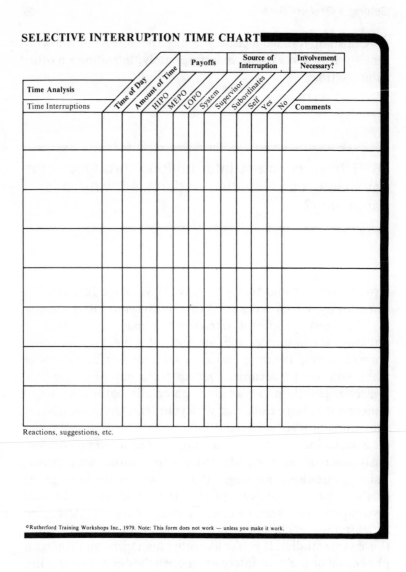

SELECTIVE INTERRUPTION TIME CHART

Time Analysis Time Interruptions	Time of Day	Amount of Time	HIPO	MEPO	LOPO	System	Supervisor	Subordinates	Self	Yes	No	Comments

Payoffs: HIPO, MEPO, LOPO
Source of Interruption: System, Supervisor, Subordinates, Self
Involvement Necessary?: Yes, No

Reactions, suggestions, etc.

Figure 4 Selective interruption time chart.

Time interruptions   List the interruptions you want to monitor. Choose one or two, such as drop-ins, phone calls, or staff conflicts.

Amount of time   Log the amount of time spent on each interruption. You don't need a stop watch, but note when the meeting began and ended or approximately how long a conversation lasted. Include also time lost (if any) in resentment or difficulty getting back to what you were doing. And don't forget the time you spend complaining about your interruption to listeners who couldn't do anything about it if their lives depended on it.

Payoffs   Indicate whether you feel the interruption was a high payoff (HIPO), medium payoff (MEPO), or low payoff (LOPO). You may want to postpone filling in this column until the end of the day or until you've had time to assess the contribution the interruption made to a valued goal. Sometimes the answer isn't always clear, but getting into the habit of questioning the value of an interruption can pay high dividends. Also, you may want to consult your scorekeepers (boss, co-workers, clients) for their viewpoint on a particular interruption. They may see something of value that you overlooked.

Source of interruption   Jot down the source of the interruption, using one or more of the four S's:

$S1$ = System-generated interruption. The system can be either internal (co-workers, organizational policies, procedures, red tape) or external (clients, governmental regulations, codes, community groups, vendors).

$S2$ = Supervisor. Your immediate boss.

$S3$ = Subordinates. The individuals directly responsible to you and those reporting to you.

$S4$ = Self. Self-generated interruptions, including restless-
ness, preoccupation, breaking your own train of thought,
fatigue, anger, illness, and so forth.

Involvement necessary Was your involvement necessary?
Was the interruption appropriate? Lots of interruptions are
necessary—in fact, some are vital. Interruptions may be the
name of your game.

Analyze each interruption to see if it could have been
screened out, delegated, postponed, shortened, or handled
differently. Perhaps it wouldn't have been a time waster if it
had come later in the day, when you weren't working to meet a
deadline. In fact, it may, at the time, have been a good use of
your time.

If you see many no's in Column V, priorities need
reassessing, practices or procedures need to be questioned, or
agreements need to be renegotiated. No's in this column are red
flags warning you to stop, look, revise, and take action.

Resist blaming others for interruptions—more often than
not, responsibility lies with you. There are many ways you
sabotage your own sincere efforts to control interruptions.
This happens when you

- Are not clear about where you time is really going.
- Are not clear about the agreements you have with yourself
  and others.
- Use the interruption as a way to avoid doing the work for
  which you are responsible.
- Indiscriminately encourage people to call or drop by to see
  you.
- Become comfortable with interruptions.
- Use them to satisfy a need to feel important or helpful.
  (After all, a person who has all these interruptions must be
  important, right?)

- Are not committed to specific goals.
- Fail to say no when you could and should say no.

Comments   Write the messages you receive from these data, such as:

- I haven't properly defined my role and responsibilities with those who interrupt me.
- I need to be conscious of the agreements between me and my interrupters. I may be saying, "It's okay to break in on me whenever you like. I'll never stand up for myself."
- I haven't delegated enough responsibility to my subordinates, so they have to get my approval on practically everything.
- I am simply available to the wrong people too much of the time.
- I don't respect my time enough to convince others to respect it.
- It's possible I haven't been careful enough of other people's time, so they don't respect mine.
- I'm not available to the right people enough of the time.

Add to this list as observations or insights occur to you. If appropriate, ask your scorekeepers how they see your interruption problems. Seek out supportive individuals to give you additional data on what is happening with your time.

Time Strategies

Experience is not what happens to you; it is what you do with what happens to you.

Aldous Huxley, *Reader's Digest,* March, 1956

"Why are you standing here on this street corner wildly waving your hands and shouting?"—"I'm keeping away the elephants."—"But there aren't any elephants here."—"You bet; that's why I'm here."

Anonymous

This chapter picks up where the last one left off, giving specific help for handling paperwork, correspondence, telephone calls, and meetings. Again, as emphasized throughout this book, remember that none of this advice works. That is, there is nothing magical or mystical about any of these techniques, and none of them work—unless you make them work.

They do work, depending—depending on the appropriateness of the strategy, depending on the circumstances and timing, depending on you. What I find valuable and effective may not be useful to you. What will work for you may not work for someone else. What worked today may not work tomorrow. What worked for you in the past may be just what you shouldn't be doing today.

In short, there are no guarantees. Keep an open mind and see how you can use these strategies, how you can modify them to fit your own specific situation.

---

37 How can I get more things done in the same amount of time? I am under constant pressure.

Your question indicates that you not only want to increase the quantity of what you accomplish but also want to improve the quality. Here are some strategies to consider.

After you have determined what your goals are, identify those activities that, when performed well, make a high contribution to your goals   These are the high payoffs (HIPOs), the vital activities that make the difference. You must make time for these activities if you are to actualize your goals. All other activities and time expenditures should relate to the support of this effort.

Establish an acceptable level of performance for what you do.   All activities generally have acceptable levels of performance. To exceed the acceptable level of performance, particularly at the low-payoff (LOPO) level, is probably to misspend your time. If you find yourself spending more time than is necessary on filing, routine tasks, standard reports, or other LOPOs, your time is probably being misused even though the task is completed better than is necessary.

Avoid the trap of diminishing returns   Even with high-payoff activities, there is a diminishing return in spending time on something beyond a certain point. While 90% of the result can be obtained by a 20% investment of time, an attempt to get an additional 5% result might require you to invest an additional 30 to 40% of time. Is it worth it to take that much more time to increase the result from 90% to 95%—especially when 90% was perfectly acceptable? Take this additional 30 to 40% of time and invest it in something that will make a higher contribution to your valued goals.

Get more of what you do by leveraging or multiplying what you have already completed and can use in similar ways   For instance, if you have researched a problem, you can of course use this information in compiling the required report. But also use it to make recommendations or write an article for your organization's newsletter. Get as much mileage as you profitably can out of what you have already done. This allows you to do more in the same amount of time.

Develop standard ways of doing things and minimize the thinking that has to go into each activity Using standard form paragraphs can expedite writing correspondence, processing requests, or completing reports. Almost anything that you do on a regular basis can lend itself to some standardization, saving time and helping to get more work out.

Look for ways of doing two needed activities at the same time For example, if you want to spend more time with your youngsters and also want to find time for physical exercise, work out with the family. Try jogging, training with weights, swimming together. You get the benefits of doing something together and getting good exercise. Similarly, instead of always having a one-on-one meeting with each of your subordinates, have a group meeting to save time and enhance communcation and teamwork. If you have to travel, it may be a good use of time and money to take along one of your staff or a member of your family in order to optimize time.

Determine more efficient ways of doing what needs to be done Perhaps a step could be reduced or eliminated that wouldn't affect the end results. Efficiency experts often are helpful in determining the best work methods to apply to the job at hand.

---

38   Why do I always seem to be under a ton of paperwork and what can I do about it?

In most cases, cutting down paperwork doesn't impair professional effectiveness and may actually improve it. Although there are as many reasons for excessive paperwork as there are people, some are common. Here is a sampling:

1   There is no self-destruct mechanism built into most tasks, so paperwork that at one time was necessary continues to be done even though it is no longer needed.

2   Form frequently overwhelms substance in committee reports, office procedures, sign-in sheets, and other "official" work. The excessive paperwork generated is not challenged because the form is often considered "beyond question."

3   Excessive paperwork allows you to feel busy, takes up time, and is comprehensible and measurable. A steady flow gives a false sense of security and accomplishment.

4   Doing paperwork can become a substitute for doing what you are really being paid to do. And you can blame your failure to do your job on all the paperwork you are required to do.

5   Doing it compensates for inadequate personal or organizational skills, conceals problem areas, and delays the need to take on more challenging and potentially higher-payoff activities.

6   It's easier to manage paper than people.

7   Paperwork is the lifeblood of bureaucracy. Higher-ups require documentation, charts require statistics, files require records. Management rewards measurable accomplishments like complete files, comprehensive records, prompt communication, and other paper-related tasks.

8   Paperwork creates the illusion of communication. Departments "talk" to departments and companies "talk" to companies through memos, reports, letters, fliers, questionnaires, and chatty newsletters.

Breaking the Paper Blockade

Encourage others to trim their paperwork as you are trimming yours. Ask subordinates for an inventory of their files and lists of the memos and reports they receive. Compare lists for duplication and transfer all duplicated material to a central file monitored and maintained by the clerical staff. A central file saves paper and copying expenses, filing and typing time, and the routing and review time spent by each sender and receiver. Here are some other ways to reduce excessive correspondence:

- Distribute only what is necessary.
- Instead of sending out several copies of correspondence, route one copy through several people.
- When routing a letter to colleagues, make appropriate remarks in the margin before you pass it on. A fast, legible, handwritten note is often an improvement over dictated and typed correspondence. It saves time and adds a personal touch that is lost on the typewriter.
- Handwritten notes encourage brevity and concise language. Too many executives express themselves poorly and waste the time of those who must wade through unnecessary and confusing prose. Handwritten notes also speed replies. They don't sit in an in-box waiting for attention.
- When appropriate, write your response to a letter at the bottom or in the margin, copy it for your records, and send the original back as your reply. When you write in the margins, stamp an explanation, such as, "We want to answer your request immediately, so please excuse the informality of our response."
- Indicate when no reply is needed to your correspondence. Needless replies waste everyone's time.

- Use form letters and modified form letters. While they're not personal or impressive, they provide fast and concise information that is often more valuable than a personalized letter. Or use speed-letter forms—the three-part speed notes combining message, response, and a copy. These save typing and filing time, encourage a rapid reply, and keep related correspondence together.

---

39   I waste too much time handling and rehandling paper that crosses my desk.

Handling a piece of paper only once is a direct and effective way to cope with all the paperwork on your desk. This means that each time you pick up a piece of paper, you make a decision that helps move it to its ultimate destination. For example:

When...	*Then...*
You have professional journals on your desk that have gone unread for weeks,	Delegate the reading to one of your staff with a note asking that he or she underline any material that you should be aware of. Delegating reading can save time, particularly if subordinates or your secretary might be reading the material anyway.

When...	*Then...*
You have a backlog of correspondence on your desk, much of it routine,	Write your answer in the margin of the letter, make a copy, and send the original back. When you want to type a completely new letter, make notes on the original for your secretary to type from.
You are responsible for summarizing a report but haven't received pertinent financial data,	Give it to your secretary with a note to return it with the financial data by a certain date.

Taking action at once is an efficient way to keep the paper moving across your desk. It can work for you when you make it work, but it does require determination and discipline. As one manager said, "Now when I open mail or go through my in-box, I don't delay my decisions. Acting now keeps my desk clear and saves time."

---

40 What can I do to save time and increase understanding in my correspondence?

By cleaning up your writing, you'll save yourself and your readers a lot of time. Here are some strategies:

- Review your memos, letters, and other writing and compare them with what comes across your desk from others. Are yours as clear and concise as you'd wish?

- Since it takes longer to write and understand a negative statement, write positive ones. Compare, for example, "Many executives don't know it is not the best practice to phrase communications in the negative, because people tend not to understand them" with "Many executives know it's smart to phrase communications positively, because people understand them better."
- Keep correspondence as brief as possible, cutting out superfluous words and phrases. Whoever said "If I had had more time, I would have written a shorter letter" understood that writing clearly is a skill which requires a lot of practice and attention.
- Use simple words. Generally, short, commonly understood words are preferable to longer, unnecessarily high-flown ones. Bring life and variety into your writing and challenge your reader with phrasing that clarifies rather than obscures meaning.
- Use an editor if you need one. Try your secretary, a colleague, your spouse, or a professional editor.
- Say what you mean. Don't make your reader interpret vague references and suggestions or sarcastic and cleverly indirect prose.
- Purge your writing of jargon, platitudes, and doubletalk.
- Use the dictionary.

---

41   I waste a lot of time waiting for others to respond to my correspondence. How can I expedite a prompt reply?

This problem can often be reduced by implementing one or more of the following techniques.

- Keep a copy of your letter to send with a handwritten note at the bottom saying "Have we missed your reply?" or "Is there something we can do for you to speed your answer?" One firm reported that over 80% of these second letters produced immediate responses.

- Suggest that correspondents write their reply at the bottom or on the back of your letter. One company found it useful to reserve lined space at the bottom of the page for replies.

- Use speed-reply forms. Write the message and keep a copy. Send the other two copies out, one for your correspondent to keep and the other to send back with his or her answer.

- Include self-addressed, stamped envelopes. They cost more, but quick replies may be worth it.

- Whenever you don't expect or need an answer, say so. Note at the bottom of the page "No reply necessary" or "For your information." Be clear about what you want and you are more likely to get it.

---

42 Misdirected telephone calls continually interrupt my day. What can I do about them?

If you think that you receive an excessive number of misdirected telephone calls, the source of the problem may lie in the following:

It Is Not Clear Where the Telephone Interruptions Are Stemming From or How Many There Are

Use some kind of a telephone record book and write down each telephone interruption as it occurs. After a few days, review when the calls come in, their sources, relevance, and the time spent on the phone. Look for the trends. Is there a special caller or group of callers? Could they be handled by the receptionist? If so, how would they be handled? Don't assume that you know all this information until you have actually completed this telephone call log. You may be surprised at what the data tells you and how useful it can be.

Telephone Calls Could Have Been Screened More Effectively but Weren't

Look at your screening agreements. Is it generally clear what you want screened? Does the screener (secretary, telephone receptionist, answering service) have your backing and the authority and responsibility needed for screening? Is the person competent and committed to screening? Give the screener specific telephone numbers and extensions of individuals who can handle misdirected phone calls.

The data you collect might indicate the calls are coming from misinformation given by the office switchboard. Or perhaps an organizational representative has been suggesting (incorrectly) to clients that you are the person to contact regarding the firm's specific product. Your phone number might be confused with someone else's. There might even be an improper listing in the telephone directory.

Misdirected phone callers not only waste your time but theirs as well, so you do everyone a favor by correcting the situation. You might ask the callers how your number was obtained. This often provides excellent data for determining why you received the phone call in the first place, instead of the person they were attempting to reach.

43   How can I avoid wasting so much time returning phone calls to people who aren't in?

This "ping pong" effect of calls out and calls in can be greatly reduced if not entirely eliminated by applying the following techniques:

When the person you are calling is not in, and you want to avoid a call back to you—

- Ask whoever answers the phone when the best time to contact that person is. Try to get specific information.
- If appropriate, leave a message with the secretary, stating your name and the purpose of the call.
- Ask if you can speak to the person's secretary, administrative assistant, or co-worker—these individuals may be able to handle the purpose of your call. At least they will be closer to the caller and can suggest ways of getting hold of him or her.
- Ask if the person you are calling can be paged. When the secretary or receptionist says, "I am sorry, Ms. Rogers is not in, can she return the call?" Ms. Rogers may be simply down the hall talking with a co-worker or out for just a few moments.
- Ask the secretary to find out what you need to know from her boss, and ask her if she would relay the information to your secretary, thereby saving her boss's time and your own.

When the person you are calling is not in and you want him or her to call you back—

- Give as much helpful information to the secretary as you can, in order to encourage the person to call you back. When there is no information, no specific time to call back, no organization name, and no informing message, people do not respond as well to the "while you were out" message.
- Give a specific time that you will be available for the telephone call. "I will be in the office from 9:45 to 11:00 A.M. and in the afternoon from 2:00 to 4:00 P.M."
- Make a telephone appointment for a specific time (such as 3:00 P.M.), a time that you have committed either to have the call returned or for you to call again. Many use the telephone appointment and treat it as if it were an appointment with the person in their office. The only difference is that it is on the phone.
- Make it attractive for the person to call you back. If you are attempting to sell something not necessarily wanted, like life insurance, tickets to the policeman's ball, or a chance to win a round-trip ticket to Siberia, this may be difficult. Plant a seed of curiosity, spell out the rewards of returning the call. You could indicate that you have a friend in common, that you have a common interest (like Little League baseball), or that someone recommended you call this person.
- Sincerely respect and encourage the support of the secretary. Let the secretary know how much you appreciate her role and support. Suggest how you can help her manager and why it is worth her manager's time to return this call. Be in the business of supporting and paying attention to the staff of the individuals you contact. They can and often do make or break your relationship to their managers.

44   How can we make better use of our meetings? Often they are boring and a waste of time.

Although meetings can save time and enhance organizational productivity, all too often they are boring time wasters. The following suggestions address common meeting problems:

If Meetings Are Too Long

Before the next meeting starts mutually determine what time it will end, and then end it at that time. Some people purposely schedule meetings to coincide with natural termination times; that is, just before lunch, closing time, or another meeting.

If Your Meetings Do Not Start on Time

Check out the hidden agreements. Nine times out of ten there is an invisible agreement that says "It's okay to start these meetings late" or "Our meetings don't really begin until the last person (or the boss, or the most important person) arrives." If the agreement is not acceptable to you, renegotiate it to get a firm new agreement with the meeting's participants about the starting time.

If the Purpose of the Meeting Isn't Clear or If Too Much Time Is Spent on One Subject

Clarify the purpose with others before the meeting. Develop and distribute the agenda and establish firm time limits for each subject to be discussed. Assign a time limit to everyone on the agenda who intends to speak.

When You Decide (or Someone Decides for You) to Attend a Meeting

- Do your homework before the meeting. Jot down notes on the agenda and organize your thoughts so that you don't waste others' time.
- Require others to do their homework before the meeting. If they are not prepared, suggest the meeting be postponed until they are.
- Be there on time and be ready to go. This conveys to other participants your commitment to getting things started on schedule.
- Take personal responsibility for making the meeting as productive as possible. Participate in ways that fulfill both the purpose of the meeting and your own needs.

When Minutes (or Notes) of the Meeting Are Desired

Save time after the meeting by writing the minutes (or your notes) before you leave the room. Give a legible outline to your secretary right away. This eliminates procrastination and the time-consuming and frustrating start-up period caused by cold notes and inertia. It also gets the minutes out to the appropriate people in time to be of value.

Eliminating Personal Time Barriers

I am a prisoner of hope when I hope someone is going to make me do for me what I must choose to do for myself.

Time Effectiveness Workshop participant

I now know that I am my own biggest time waster and until I come to grips with that reality few if any personal time barriers will be eliminated.

Time Effectiveness Workshop participant

You hold the key to gaining more out of your time by using the enormous power you have to manage yourself and your time. Unfortunately, most of us fail too often in making the best use of our time—blocked by personal time barriers.

In a certain sense, we have all been unconscious fools in many of the ways we have chosen to manage our time. We all make excuses for not getting the most out of our time, we have all entered into "invisible" agreements that have, in effect, invited others to dump into our Wheelbarrows of Time.

The questions/responses in this chapter focus on such concerns as overcoming self-defeating excuses, developing ways of breaking through procrastination, and gaining momentum through taking responsible initiative. The underlying premise in each case is that you have the power to take responsibility for yourself and for your time, and that you can use it—just in time.

---

45   Why do I seem to find so many excuses for not doing what I know I should do?

This is all too common for most of us. There are many activities—such as planning, reevaluating our goals, clearing up an important but confused relationship, taking time to be with a loved one—that are unnecessarily and repeatedly postponed. Whatever these potentially high-payoff activities (HIPOs) are, if you find that you are continually not doing them, you may be trapped by your own excuses.

Listed here are some of the more common ones.

I don't have time   Deferred HIPOs are by definition those activities that you have not acted on but *do* have time to do, activities that you could, should, and would do if you were managing your time effectively. Therefore the problem is one of making time, and you are an unconscious fool for not doing so and for continuing to say, "I don't have time to do them." To be a fool is human, but you don't have to be a practicing fool.

I'll have time to do it later   This is probably more insidious than the previous excuse because nothing will make you do your HIPO tomorrow when you could have, should have, and would have done it today but didn't. There is nothing wrong with saying "Friday is a better time for me to take the inititiative on this HIPO" if, in fact, you are going to do it Friday. But if you continually and habitually say you will do it tomorrow and don't, then you are kidding yourself.

I will do it whenever . . .   Whenever the phones stop ringing, whenever people stop dropping by for short conversations, whenever I don't have to attend all those meetings or make out all those financial reports. Whenever I don't have to pick up my car from the garage, drop the children off at the dentist, or go to the doctor, I will find time to do my deferred, unactualized HIPO. But when when does "whenever" happen? Never, unless you make it happen.

Convincing yourself that you will really do a HIPO, when in fact you won't, is to delude yourself. You are waiting for something to happen, for a time when all the other things in your life stop hitting you and demanding your time and attention. This will never happen. The sooner you stop thinking you will do it "whenever," the sooner you will actually do it.

I could do it if they would just stop doing it to me   Blame is the perfect excuse for not taking action on what you could and should do: blame takes the responsibility off your back and puts it on the back of someone else. "They—if they (whoever they might be) would just stop messing things up for me, I would be able to find time to do my deferred HIPO." Does that sound familiar? It is easy to blame others for our own failings or failure to manage our time and life.

All blame does is transfer responsibility for doing your HIPO from you, where it belongs, to whomever you are blaming: it puts *them* in control of your time. If I allow myself to blame by boss for my inability to meet my deadlines, or blame my secretary for continually allowing interruptions to interfere with my work, or blame my co-workers for not following through on their part of the project, then I don't seem responsible for failing to get my job done.

Inevitably there will be times when others hinder your ability to get your work done, but that isn't what we're referring to. The blame we are talking about here is the kind that inappropriately shifts the focus of responsibility for managing your time from yourself to others.

Check yourself the next time you find yourself saying, "I would be able to do my HIPOs if they would stop fouling me up. I would be able to sit down and really plan the next four months and establish some meaningful goals. I would be able to find time to work more closely with my secretary/administrative assistant to ensure that we are on the same wave frequency. But (ah, there is the qualifier) *they* are doing it to me. My boss is doing it to me, my co-workers are doing it to me, the world is doing it to me... and if they would just stop, then I could find time for my HIPOs." Forget it. They never did it to you and, even if they did, they would never stop doing it just because you blamed them.

I can't   This excuse is used to convince yourself that you can't do the HIPO activity, even though you actually can. You can put yourself down by saying, "I don't have the necessary skills, understanding, or Ph.D degree. I wasn't born on the right side of town, my color is not right, and I am too short." But this kind of statement is usually nothing more than a smoke screen, camouflage thrown up to convince yourself (and perhaps others) that you can't do something. If you truly don't have the necessary skills, understanding, or resources right now, you can put a high priority on acquiring them. But you can do so only when you stop saying "I can't." "I can't" just won't get the job done for you.

We are only talking here about those activities that you *can* do but have, for a number of self-defeating reasons, chosen to tell yourself you can't do. Activities that you cannot in fact do are not included. For example, if you want to be a professional basketball player and you are five feet two inches tall, forty years old, have heart disease, and one leg is shorter than the other, then perhaps you have reason to say "I can't." In that case a HIPO for you would be to understand that this basketball player HIPO you have been deferring is simply a fantasy that is blocking your ability to manage your life realistically (not to mention being crazy).

I wish I could figure out what I really want to do with my time and life   You cannot puposefully act on a HIPO when you don't know what your valued goals are. HIPOs are those activities that make a high contribution to the reaching of your goals—and without goals there is no way for you to determine what your HIPOs even are. Therefore, "wishing" prevents you from clarifying those goals.

I am waiting for someone to help me   Waiting for a rescuer to help you to do the high-payoff activities that you are responsible for is hopeless. Being a practicing prisoner of hope—hoping that somehow, someone will come to your rescue and get you to do what only you can do for yourself—undermines your responsibility for yourself and keeps you from acting on your HIPOs. Only you can take the initiative to give priority to high-payoff activities in your work and life. Only you can present your ideas to management, move to clear up your personal resentment with a co-worker, or be motivated to excel in your work. No one can make you do it. There is no Santa Claus, no Fairy Godmother, no Big Rescuer in the Sky. Waiting for your rescuer is sad, hopeless, and unproductive, and it seduces you into believing that someone else will assume responsibility for those actions that only you can undertake.

I'll try "Trying" to do your HIPOs is setting yourself up for another excuse not to do them. When you hear yourself say "I will try to find time to plan" or "I will try to find time to spend with my family" or "I will try to find time to work more closely with my subordinates," you can almost always translate this to mean: "I will try. I won't find time, but I will have the excuse of 'Well, I tried.'" You will either find time to plan, to spend time with your family, and to help your subordinates, or you will not. Stop "trying" to find time for those deferred HIPOs, just do them.

---

46 How can I tell whether I am procrastinating or merely being correctly cautious?

Sometimes you can't be sure: too many situations lack certainties and guarantees. But there are some guidelines to help you to tell the difference.

What is procrastination? You are procrastinating when you

inappropriately put off doing something that you could do now, should do now, and would do now if you were to manage yourself and your time more responsibly and effectively.

Could Do Now

In order to be considered procrastinating, you must be *able* to do the activity that you are putting off now. You are not procrastinating if you cannot do it, either for lack of time, skill, knowledge, or opportunity. You may be inappropriately putting off gaining the skills, time, knowledge, or opportunity necessary for doing this task, but you are not procrastinating on the task itself.

Should Do Now

You must also feel that you *should* do it now, that it is something worthwhile, appropriate, and timely for you to do. Should implies that the time is right. Does it make more sense to do the task now or later? You must weigh the evidence and decide. However, if, after due consideration, you think you both should and could tackle your HIPO now but are not, you more than likely are procrastinating.

Would Do Now

The third criterion of procrastination is whether you *would* do it now. Whereas *could* deals with capability and *should* deals with desirability, *would* focuses on your intent and will to take action—the intention to decide to stop putting off the task and do it. Tasks that you could and should do now don't get done when you lack the will to decide to take action.

Listed below are some additional characteristics of procrastination.

It's a disadvantage to wait   If the time is right for action now, either because you will lose the opportunity if you wait or because there is a clear advantage to acting immediately, you are procrastinating by waiting. It is easy to persuade yourself that you are correctly delaying action until more information is available, or until conditions are right. But, in fact, all these considerations may merely be smokescreens to avoid the responsibility and risk entailed in acting *now*.

Energy and time are being needlessly drained from you   Fretting and frustration are common results of procrastination. Another good indication that you are procrastinating instead of being wisely cautious is your feeling about the inaction. If you feel guilty and worry, the chances are good that you are procrastinating.

Your "reasons" and "excuses" don't hold water   Take a hard look at what you tell yourself about your inaction. Become a "third neutral party," step back, and see how they stand up. Are you saying the following?

"I don't have time to do it now."

"I will do it later when the time is better."

"I can't do it."

"I could do it if they would just let me, but they always get in my way."

"I never really had a chance. Circumstances were just against me."

---

47   How can I break through my procrastination?

Here are some strategies that have helped others.

Divide and Conquer

The technique of taking what seems to be an insurmountable task and dividing it into more workable parts is as old as humankind. If you want to write a book of 300 pages, it can seem like an overwhelming task. But if you divide the work into manageable parts and write 400 carefully chosen words a day, you'll have yourself a book in six months. Try to see each part that you have divided the task into as whole—to be started and completed in one step. Each step, then, will add to the previous one and lead to the completion of your total task.

When the mountain climber Sir Edmund Hillary was asked how he became the first man in history to climb Mt. Everest, he said that he never saw the mountain as a whole but rather saw it in stages. Each stage was planned for completion in one day. And by completing stage after stage, day after day, he conquered the unconquerable Mt. Everest. The wisdom of the adage "the longest journey begins with a single step" is clear.

Start with a Part That Is Believable

If you are procrastinating doing something because it is too large to take on or seems too difficult, or because you feel you can't do it, select a part of the activity that you think is possible to complete. By starting at this point, you will break through your inertia and gain the momentum to help carry you to at least partial completion of your task. When you believe it is too large a task to take on, it is. Go with the part that you believe you can begin and complete, and the momentum gained will help you to conquer your resistance to act on the whole.

Make a Game of Doing It

Some of the things that we put off are tedious and seemingly unrewarding, but they still need to be done. Such things as filling out IRS income data for an accountant, taking the car to the garage to have it repaired, reading government regulations, checking over certain reports, and handling routine correspondence are all likely to excite one as much as boring, smoke-filled meetings.

But you can make a game out of it and find new ways of doing the task. In the case of routine, unexciting paperwork, see how much you can do in twenty minutes and keep a record of your progress. See if there are new ways you can process the paper. Become interested in how the paper that you complete is used, if at all. You might even work at becoming an expert in one aspect of the handling of paperwork. One manager who chose to make a game out of his paperwork became well informed on the history of some of the company reports—how they came about, their original purpose, and how they are being used today, if at all, by the company. While not a company historian, he could certainly spin interesting yarns about what he learned while researching those reports.

Seven and Eleven It

Give the procrastinated task seven minutes, and seven minutes only, in the morning. Then, in the afternoon, give it eleven minutes—no more and no less. Clock yourself when you use this technique and, even if you are in the middle of the project when the time is up, stop. On the next day during the seven- and eleven-minute cycles, if you find that you want to continue investing more time after the seven minutes are up, go ahead.

The key point on the first go-around is to know that you will not spend more than eighteen minutes (out of the 1,440 minutes in any given day) on this procrastinated task.

Build in Accountability

First, determine how much of the procrastinated task you are willing to be held accountable for; then draw up a self-starting contract that specifies not only what you have agreed to do but also spells out the consequences if you fail to do it. Or, as an alternative, give your accountability to someone to hold for you. Take, for example, a supervisor who finds it difficult to find the time to meet with his subordinates for quarterly performance reviews, even though he knows the review could play an important part in team development. He asks his immediate boss to hold him accountable for these meetings, and they draw up an agreement outlining the rewards and penalties for this task. This formalizing of the task clarifies its significance and greatly simplifies the problem of getting it done.

Make It Ridiculous

Choose an aspect of the procrastinated task that is easy to do but that you are still putting off because you don't like to do it. Now, make the doing of this task (in your mind) as ridiculous as possible. If the task is writing a letter of acknowledgment that would take twenty-five minutes, blow up the letter-writing and visualize it in a way that makes it laughable. For example, can you see thousands and thousands of people waiting breathlessly for you to perform the monumental and earth-shaking task of writing this letter? Or perhaps you can see your correspondent waiting for it with a wheelbarrow of $1000 bills for you.

What does this accomplish? It not only makes the job more amusing, but also heightens your awareness of what it is that you are procrastinating.

Reward Yourself BIG

Choose a part of the procrastinated task that you have been putting off. Perhaps it is nothing more than making an outline of a report that is due in three weeks or getting information on enrolling in graduate school. Then, decide that upon com-

pleting part of the procrastinated task, you will reward yourself
BIG. Make the reward so great (or the penalty so severe) that
you have no other option than to do the task.

   In her newly assigned managerial role in a major bank,
Sheila found every reason, every excuse, for not confronting a
real office problem that had developed between two of her
subordinates and herself. The situation was becoming embar-
rassing for her boss and for the other office personnel. So
Sheila called both subordinates in separately, presented them
with the problem as she saw it, and outlined some of the
options available to them if they felt they couldn't work for her
as their new manager. After the uncomfortable yet necessary
confrontation, Sheila rewarded herself with an elaborate
dinner with a friend and then took a two-day sailing vacation
she had been wanting to take for a long time. The reward Sheila
promised herself was exciting enough to motivate her to break
through her procrastination.

Put It on Automatic

Jason M. was continually putting off going to the gym to
exercise. He was thirty-seven and eight inches too big around
the waist; his chest had simply slipped to his waist. He felt out
of condition, his energy was low, and his work was being
affected. For him, thinking about going to the gym or taking
time to swim, run, or play tennis was burdensome. He had as
much interest in fitness as he had in piano moving.

   So he put his fitness program on automatic pilot: he didn't
think about working out, he didn't imagine what the rewards
might be, he didn't divide and conquer anything, he didn't even
make a game of it. he just did it—without thinking. He made a
routine of automatically working out at 6:00 P.M. every
Monday and Thursday and he never stopped to ask, "Should I
or shouldn't I? What are the pros and cons of doing this?" He
just did it. He still doesn't like working out but he does it
nevertheless.

Managers have activated their automatic robots for such things as filling out their expense forms, getting weekly reports in, calling two new clients per day, or making one customer-relations appointment per day.

David and Goliath It

With this technique, you simply face the problem squarely. There are probably really tough assignments you just don't want to do and that are easily put off. Nevertheless, they have to be done. So David and Goliath them. See yourself as a young protector of the faith, a David going to battle with an unpleasant, obnoxious, and obstinate giant. Confront and defeat your imagined giant and feel the triumphant vibrations of victory.

---

48   How can I learn to take more initiative, both in my personal and in my professional life?

To take the initiative is to take the first step, to turn an idea or a thought into reality through action. It is to make something happen that would not otherwise happen. If your manager suggests that you take more initiative, he or she is inviting you to act more often on your own without checking first. Your manager may be saying that he or she wants you to do more primary decision making, to be self-motivated, or to take action without waiting for others to prompt you.

The initiative process is characterized by the following:

Action-taking rather than passive waiting for something to happen   Taking initiative implies a desire to make things happen, a willingness to take action and be responsible for it. It is recognizing what needs to be done and then moving to accomplish it. If your manager has to continually point out tasks that need your attention, opportunities that should be taken, and concerns you need to address, your value as a team member is greatly diminished.

Willingness to move from the known (the status quo) to the unknown   It is so easy to get stuck in the way things are, even when you really don't want them to remain that way. Part of the initiative process is giving up the known for the unknown: taking the first steps into a different environment and risking failure in exchange for the thrilling possibility of success.

Independence rather than dependence   Initiators take action on their own. They do not always wait for others' suggestions or approval, but are willing to be responsible for their actions and make independent judgments. They do not require others' approval or rely heavily on someone else but act on their own.

More emphasis on risk than security   Part of the initiative process is chancing that the specific initiative fails completely, but initiators will keep a margin of security. They may risk $10,000 in a business venture, but not $100,000. They are calculated-risk takers, weighing the advantages and disadvantages of the risk. It often seems safer not to take the initiative—not to move to clear up misunderstandings, not to question policy, not to tread new ground, not to experience and test new ways of viewing, thinking, feeling, and acting on things. But it is generally far less rewarding, and you thereby take another risk: the gamble that you will suffer the immeasurable loss of what might have been yours had you taken the risk.

Expansion rather than restriction   The enterprising person will broaden horizons, will search for new opportunities, and will be on the lookout for innovative and more productive ways of improving his or her environment. Possibilities for growing through taking initiative include expanding your expectations, attitudes, and knowledge, as well as establishing new standards for yourself.

Concern with opportunities to assist and support, and deemphasis of personal rights   While not denying the importance of standing up for your rights, initiative taking at times puts your rights secondary to getting the job done. It might not be right for your manager to ask you to stay late to work on a project due in two days, especially when it would have been unnecessary to work overtime had he planned ahead. But in order to get the job done, you should be able to subordinate your rights, at least temporarily. Initiators are also willing to seek out opportunities to initiate tasks, even when those activities are not in their job descriptions.

Greater willingness to take the extra step   This is closely aligned to seeking opportunities to assist and support. I remember my high school football coach, who was stronger on homilies than football technique, saying, "If all of you do your share, there will always be one share left undone." If no one takes the extra step beyond just what he or she is paid to do and is being held accountable for, there will always be "one share left undone."

---

49   I feel like I am in a rut, not only in my work but in my personal life. How can I at least try to get out?

It's easy to get into ruts, in all aspects of our lives. It's easy for us to become prisoners of the past, locked into outdated, ineffective patterns. Breaking out of ruts becomes much easier when we recognize and acknowledge that part of the reason we are in those ruts in the first place is because we "got used to them." By carefully reviewing your habits and routines, you can discover why you take too much time, upset your tempo, or accomplish nothing.

Here are some tips.

Find new ways to look at the same problems Deliberately go out of your way to break with the old order. It may help to change even some of your "simple" habits. Try taking a different route to work, eating at a different restaurant, and choosing a different meal.

Concentrate To break out of your rut, increase your awareness of what's going on around you. When your tempo has begun to drop, a quick way to snap out of it is by concentrating on something, such as the way the flowers are arranged or the way a piece of furniture is put together. A little concentration can be refreshing, open new vistas for you, and break the ho-hum of your old, preoccupied way of doing things. Concentrating creates energy that can be used to challenge the mindless-rut routines you find yourself locked into.

Observe Closely linked to concentrating is simply observing what is happening around you. One of the problems of falling into ruts is that we tend to lose our attention. Start noticing things in your immediate environment, things that have generally gone unnoticed before. Take a walk and look at people and how they move, talk, and act. Listen to the sounds of the city. Notice things that you have never bothered to look at before because you have been so caught in your own rut.

Increase your knowledge A job routine (even your entire job) can become a habit, a nonthinking, almost robotlike way of conducting yourself from 8:00 A.M. to 5:00 P.M. Take a new interest in learning all you can about your job and related work. Are you as knowledgeable about what you do as a doctor is about medicine or a physicist is about physics? Are you a pro in understanding the various aspects of your work— why it is important, how it is done, and what the latest techniques and discoveries are in your field? Simply learning more about your work can increase your interest, suggest new ways of doing things, and provide ways to break through the ordinary and routine of what you do.

Experiment   Seek alternate ways of doing the same thing. Try new activities. Ask yourself, "Is there a better and more effective way of doing what I am now doing?" You might eliminate some of the activities you are now doing and see what happens. Ask yourself, "What could I do that I am not doing that would be productive, worthwhile, and add to my sense of well-being— something that would make the difference?" Then experiment and do it. You will be surprised to see how easy it is to break out of some of your day-to-day ruts. You simply do not have the time to be caught up in the routine of it all when you are actively seeking new ways of working and relating and living.

Reset your goals   More people, I suspect, have problems with setting and resetting goals than they have pursuing them. When you find yourself in a rut, reevaluate what it is that you want to do with your life. What are the goals that you want to achieve in your work? What activities need to be performed for you to actualize these goals? Setting and pursuing worthwhile goals is the greatest rut cruncher available.

---

50   Why do I fail to find time for planning, even though I realize how important it is?

The answer to your question is found in the very nature of planning, which is central to winning the time game.

Planning is recognized as important but not urgent to do Few managers and professionals would argue that planning is not important: it is crucial to managing work and time. It is not *urgent,* though, in most cases; that is, the status quo can typically be maintained without long-range plans.

Here is an example. James L. faced the daily pressures of meeting this deadline, completing that task, receiving phone calls, handling paperwork, attending meetings, and all that goes with a busy day for the average manager. He knew the value of planning. He often stated that he wanted to find time to establish meaningful goals and make plans for achieving them. But in the pressure of the day, there was always something else to be done. Planning was a high payoff(HIPO) for James, but it was always deferred—it carried a low or no priority at all. Important, yes; urgent, no. All the random and routine daily activities were urgent and time critical for James to do, or at least that is how he perceived them. But planning was not.

Planning is viewed as so extremely important that the perfect time to do it never arrives Planning gets deferred when it is viewed as so important that it must have undivided attention. When will you be able to give it your full attention, the attention planning deserves? When does that ever happen? How often does it happen that you have no reports to fill out, phones to answer, people's problems to work with, meetings to attend, items to take care of, or discussions to hold? Seldom, if ever.

One manager, when asked when he would begin his postponed planning, responded, "I am going to do my essential short- and long-range planning whenever." I asked him what he meant by "whenever," and he responded, "Whenever I don't have to answer all the questions asked me by management team, or attend all the divisional meetings and special get-togethers, or handle all the bureaucratic red tape, or cover for my boss's stupid mistakes, or protect my backside so much... whenever." In short, there would never be time to plan.

You and I probably have our own special whenevers:

whenever the time is right, whenever we get motivated, whenever they stop doing it to us, whenever the great rescuer comes to save us from our time dilemma, or whenever planning becomes so important that we will actually do it. Like other deferred high payoffs (HIPOs), however, planning will never get done until you make time for it.

Planning is decision making for the future   Because planning deals with the future, it tends to be postponed or deferred until the future. Because you can't plan yesterday and can only plan for the time ahead, it is easy to get caught up in the trap of waiting until the future to plan.

Planning seems impossible because the future is unknown How can you plan one year, or five years, when things happen and change so rapidly? The only sure thing is change, and how can you plan for that? This feeling of futility is a severe barrier to effective planning. Yet in spite of the certainty of change, a well thought out and flexible plan is one of the best strategies you have toward reaching your goals.

Planning carries an inherent risk   When you plan, you state what you intend to accomplish for others to see and evaluate. With some managers, it is clear that the real deterrent to creative planning and applying that planning is the pale of risk hovering over them. Setting goals and planning their accomplishment is to risk failure.

I am sure that you could add to this list of why your planning doesn't get done, even when it is important and carries a high payoff. But one thing is clear: your planning won't get done until you give it a high priority.

Delegation: The Key To Managerial Sanity

Those who enjoy responsibility usually get it: those who merely like exercising authority usually lose it.

Malcolm Forbes

A poor delegator is in a constant time bind.

An old management saying

One of the most important—and probably the most misunderstood and abused—management skills is the art of delegation. Knowing how to delegate effectively is not just knowing how to assign work to others, but also knowing what is appropriate to assign and what tasks you should be doing. Effective delegating is necessary to prevent you from being buried in work that isn't yours and to ensure that you have the time for the work that *is* yours. It is the key to managerial sanity.

Yet delegation is difficult, and for an array of subtle reasons. Why do we fail to delegate when we know we should? How can we be sure how much authority has been delegated to us, and how much we are authorized to delegate? Where is that fine line between proper delegation and "illegal" dumping? How do we avoid "reverse delegation"?

This chapter looks at these and other delegation problems, and provides guidelines for developing your own blueprint for effective delegation.

---

51 I am continually overloaded with work and always facing time deadlines. Yet I still find it difficult to delegate work to my subordinates.

Proper delegation is the assignment to others of task responsibilities that they could, should, and would do if you were an effective manager. It is a basic and indispensable tool. The ineffective delegator is in a constant time bind, never able to get on top of the job, bogged down with nonessentials that either should be done by others or should be eliminated altogether. You may not truly acknowledge the importance of delegating. Yet if you are to be successful in managing your time, you must learn to delegate effectively—it is the secret to managerial sanity.

It is through delegation that the effective manager avoids needlessly spending large amounts of time on activities that do not require his or her personal attention, thereby freeing precious time to channel to more productive and rewarding responsibilities.

When you spend time doing activities that your subordinates and staff members should be doing, you mismanage your time. When you as a manager fail to delegate responsibility effectively, in a sense you are a thief, robbing from several sources:

1 You rob from your subordinates by not assigning them tasks that give them a chance to grow and develop their skills.
2 You rob yourself by creating a perpetual time bind in which time for important job responsibilities, new opportunities, and skills development cannot be found.
3 You rob your organization by not performing the jobs that you are being paid to perform.
4 You often rob your family by frantically trying to catch up, and by stealing time away from home to make up time lost at work.

We fail to delegate, or delegate improperly, for many reasons. We may be—

Feeling indispensable You may be thinking that only you can get the job done properly because you have the necessary skills, knowledge, experience, and personality. But then the world's graveyards are filled with people who thought themselves "indispensable." I suspect many of them found it impossible to get away from the office and find time for their families, impossible to allow others to do the jobs they were being paid to do.

Thinking "I'll do it myself."   Although someone else could do it, you may think you can do the job better, easier, faster, and more accurately than anyone else. "I'll do it myself" is an easy trap to fall into, particularly when there are occasions when it is in fact best for you to do the assignment, to write the report, to handle the direct sale, or to fix broken pieces of machinery. Ask yourself, however, whether someone else's "not so good" isn't really good enough, especially when it allows you to free up time for more important actions.

Lacking confidence in others   You lack the confidence to assign a task because you think others are incompetent or that you will be held responsible for their work. Your unwillingness to take a chance may keep you doing tasks that rightfully belong to others.

Thinking "I like to do it myself."   Doing an activity simply because you like to or because it gives you a sense of control and satisfaction can be a real trap. Is it okay for you to draw the engineering plans, to make the sales call, and to run the machine when there are more important things for you to do? Doing some of these activities on a selected, conscious basis may be appropriate, but be judicious.

Unaware that the activity should be delegated   You may be unaware that what you are now doing should be assigned to someone else. Pause once in awhile and ask yourself, "Should I delegate this activity to someone else?" Other good questions are the following: "If I were to delegate this task to someone

else, what would I accomplish? What would I get done that
isn't getting done now? What would be the effect on the person
to whom the task is delegated?"

Lacking delegation skills   You may simply not know or not
think you know how to delegate effectively. You may not be
sure how to communicate to others, how to set up and define
responsibilities and accountability; you may feel uncomfortable with your skill in negotiating agreements with subordinates. These skills can be learned.

Understaffed   You actually may not have anyone to delegate
to. If there is a permanent understaffing situation, your
management time will be seriously impaired. Immediate
corrective action, aside from pitching in and getting the work
accomplished yourself, is to call on some form of temporary
help.

Hindered by a supervisor   Your boss may verbally espouse
the need for you to delegate. But if you are constantly held
accountable for every little detail and procedure of a project
(and they seemingly become more important than the results of
the project itself), it is difficult, if not impossible, to delegate
these tasks to your subordinates properly.

Misguidedly benevolent   You may feel that you are helping
out your subordinates by doing work for them, when in fact
you could be seriously curtailing their professional growth by
limiting their opportunities to take on more substantial
assignments. Misguided benevolence comes in many forms,
such as the rescuer—"I will help you out by doing it for you";
the protector—"I will protect you from these difficult tasks";
and the good guy—"I am such a good guy I will do it for you."
A dysfunctional need to be inappropriately kind can under-
mine your managerial ability. You actually train others to rely
on you to do their job for them.

52   How can I be more aware of my responsibility to delegate?

Awareness itself is the first step in enhancing your ability to delegate. Here are some questions to ask yourself in order to increase that awareness.

Do I Delegate Appropriate Amounts of Work to My Subordinates?

Is there a proper balance between routine, "nitty-gritty" tasks and growth-promoting and challenging ones? Do you have a clear understanding with your subordinates about the what and why of each assignment? Do your subordinates view their delegated tasks as appropriate for them to handle?

Do I, When Appropriate, Require My Staff to Outline Their Best Thinking on Their Job Responsibilities?

Having subordinates outline their recommendations and understandings in summary form allows you to get to the meat of the problem immediately and helps them to crystallize their ideas. Writing clarifies the mind and encourages clear, concise thinking.

Do I Fail to Delegate to Others Due to My Misguided Benevolence, Thinking That I Am Really Helping Them Out, When, in Fact, I Am Hindering Their Development?

Giving responsibility to subordinates is not just allocating work, but also providing them with opportunities to grow and learn by doing. It can hurt to discover that you are not indispensable, that others can perform adequately without your doing for them, and it is sometimes difficult to practice the art of *not* doing for others. But it is important to realize that by refusing to do something for them, you often make their lives better.

Do I Find It Difficult to Let Go of Some of My Work?

The source of this difficulty may range from simply wanting to do it yourself to lack of confidence in your delegate, to fear of giving up part of your job. It can be difficult to give up doing what you do well and perhaps at one time were paid to do. For instance, sales managers often find it difficult not to jump in to close the sale for one of their sales staff, or an engineering manager will find it difficult not to engineer instead of manage.

Am I Clear With Others About What I Expect When I Delegate to Them?

Is there mutual agreement as to what is to be done and how and when it is to be finished? Is there a working understanding about the level of authority at which the delegate is working? How much initiative may be taken and how much reporting is necessary? Ask the delegate what he or she understands the assigned task to be and you can prevent a lot of misunderstanding and wasted time later on. What you understand as delegator and what the delegate understands may be significantly different.

Do I Recognize That I May Be Seen by My Subordinates as Dumping Into Their Wheelbarrows of Time Instead of Legitimately Delegating to Them, and Do I Seek to Clear This Up With Them?

There is no such thing as legalized dumping and no such thing as illegal delegating. Either you have the proper authority to delegate something to someone, or you do not have the authority and are guilty of illegal dumping.

There is one exception: if you should be eliminating some task altogether but instead are delegating it to a subordinate, your failure to eliminate it is, in a sense, illegal delegation. Have you, as a subordinate, ever been assigned a task that you knew should not be done at all? How did you feel? Common feelings range from, "That's the way it is, but it sure is stupid," to resentment, anger, frustration, and vengeance. In all cases, you, as a manager, are the loser. Who needs a resentful, angry, apathetic, defeated person on the team?

There is probably more misunderstanding and confusion about what is proper to delegate and what is not than any other single management practice.

Do I Have a Mutually Understood and Agreed-To Set of Guidelines for Delegating Responsibility to Others?

Getting the job done with more than one person is always a team effort. While all members of your team do not have to agree to your methods of delegating, at minimum the delegate needs to accept your delegation and treat it as if he or she agreed to it. Otherwise, you will have sabotage, insubordination, and poor results.

Do I Recognize That Generally Subordinates Will Dump as Many of Their Monkeys (Problems) on My Back as I Am Willing to Carry?

In some cases, there is no end to the number of monkeys and crises subordinates can think of to place on to the big, broad backs of their willing managers. It is almost like the manager has a huge sign on the office door saying, "Bring your problems to Big Problem Solver and I will solve them for you, my children." Parents can also suffer from monkey transference, from child to Mom and Dad.

Do I Realize That When I Inappropriately Take on My Subordinates' Problems I Become Subordinate, and They Become My "Supervisors"?

That is, your subordinate becomes a "supervisor" waiting to see how you will do on the "delegated task" he or she gave you. This problem has become your problem, and you have become a party to negative reverse delegation. One manager remarked that it had come to the point where his phone was constantly ringing with calls from his subordinates (five of them) checking up on him to see how much progress he was making on solving the problems they had handed him. They were probably eager for him to solve the current problems so they could bring him more monkeys to feed and care for. How many parents have fallen into this reverse delegation trap by taking on the youngsters' small problems instead of allowing them the challenge of solving their own?

Do I Realize That When I Delegate Something to Someone I Am Responsible For Supporting Them As Much As Possible in Performing That Particular Assignment?

Your involvement will vary depending on the assignment. You are there to assist in handling problems, but only as a resource person and not as the doer and solver of the task. This will keep the problem and task where it has been appropriately delegated and where it belongs, in the court of the subordinate.

Do I Occasionally Delegate an Activity That Should Be Relegated to the Wastebasket?

To delegate a task that should be eliminated is a waste of time—for both you and the delegate. Before delegating a doubtful task ask yourself the questions, "What would happen if no one did this task? Who would care if this task never were done? Lucky is the manager who has a team member who is willing to question needless tasks—not to make the manager wrong but to cut down and eliminate unnecessary low-payoff activities, with the purpose of freeing time for more important and higher-payoff tasks.

Do I Sometimes Ask My Subordinates or Others to Whom I Delegate, "What Am I Doing That Dumps Into Your Wheelbarrow of Time and Wastes Your Time?"

You may not be aware of something you are doing that is perceived by your subordinate as a time waster for him or her. Asking this question and truly listening to the response can give you valuable information about what your subordinates think are valid requests for their time and which ones, if any, they think waste their time.

Of course, do not ask the question unless you really want to hear the response. If you are not going to listen to what they say, you will cause more resentment and anger than if you had never asked the question. It takes, in a sense, a brave and self-assured manager to ask his or her subordinates, "What am I doing that wastes your time and prevents you from getting your job done?" If you are willing to listen to what they say, you will be a better manager for it.

---

53 I would like to have a guideline or checklist to help me delegate more effectively.

Checklists can often be helpful clarifiers. Respond to the following short delegation statements with a simple yes or no. Yes means that you generally do what is stated and no means that generally you don't. If you are not sure how you do, insert a question mark. Write any additional responses you have to the statements in the "comment" column.

If you answered "yes" to these delegation questions, you are probably delegating effectively. If you answered "no" to some of them, you have areas that need improvement. The following comments correspond to the numbered statements of the chart.

1   If you don't delegate appropriate amounts of work to your subordinates, you may be doing too much of their work

Yes	No	?	Comment	
				1 I delegate appropriate amounts of work to my subordinates.
				2 When appropriate, I ask my subordinates to outline their best thinking on a subject before they report to me.
				3 I outline what is expected when I delegate activities to others, and I clearly state the standard of performance I expect.
				4 I recognize that my subordinates sometimes may experience my delegating as dumping into their Wheelbarrows of Time, and I seek to clear this up with them.

Yes	No	?	Comment	
				5 I have established a set of rules relative to my responsibility to delegate to others, a framework that my subordinates understand and agree to.
				6 I sometimes ask subordinates, "What am I doing that dumps into your Wheelbarrow of Time and wastes your time?
				7 I encourage my subordinates to take initiative in areas not clearly spelled out, as long as they keep me properly informed.
				8 I periodically examine my delegating style to avoid falling into the trap of over- or under-delegating.

yourself, allowing work to go undone, or both. What constitutes an appropriate amount of work will vary from situation to situation, of course, and can be established by mutual negotiation and agreement.

2 Complete staff reporting from your subordinates gives you the benefit of their input and requires that they think through problems themselves. Many managers like to have a three-fourths-page summary of the contents of a staff report attached to the cover of the report, enabling them to quickly get the essential jist and recommendation of the report.

3   Often delegation fails due to a lack of communication and mutual understanding about what is to be completed. Ask your people to repeat back to you what they understand to be the delegated assignment. This will give you both an immediate opportunity to clarify any misunderstandings and to gain agreement on what is to be done. It is of little consolation to find that the wrong job has been done well, especially when this could have been prevented by taking a few extra minutes in the beginning. Have you ever heard, "Gosh, Boss, I thought you said ... ," or, "Gee, I was sure that you wanted me to ... "?

4   If you are an effective delegator, you will recognize that occasionally your subordinates may think that you are wasting their time by assigning them tasks that you have no right to assign in the first place. This perception can easily cause frustration, resentment, and even a situation in which subordinates are "getting even" with you. You may be perfectly right in assigning them a task, but if they do not see it that way, there can be serious problems ahead for you (and them). Observe and listen to what your subordinates do and say relative to the assigned task. Find out how they feel about an assignment when you suspect that there is a problem and clarify the scope of the task for them.

5   Your subordinates need to know what is expected of them and what the guidelines are for their performance of an assigned task—who is to do what, when and where, and why, and how it is to be done. This does not mean spoon-feeding your people, but it does mean outlining the ground rules and framework within which the work is to be done.

6   Unless you really want to hear what your subordinates feel you are doing that wastes their time, don't ask. And certainly don't ask unless you are willing to really listen. You don't have to agree with what they say, or do anything about it even if you do agree, but you must, at a minimum, be open to empathetically listening to their comments. What happened the last time you asked a subordinate of

yours, "What am I doing that prevents you from getting your work done?" What was the response?

7 For many managers, to encourage those who report to them to take initiative is a very difficult challenge. It is impossible to know completely what your people could and would do if they were managing themselves effectively. But when they have your confidence and support in taking initiative in certain areas, they can increase their and your contribution to getting the job done. It is important, however, that you be as clear as possible about which areas they may take initiative on and which ones you want them to check out with you first. Also, be sure that they keep you properly informed.

8 If you don't continually observe your delegating style (or in some cases, your nondelegating style), you can easily fall into the many traps of poor delegation that were mentioned earlier. Recognize that when you are a poor delegator, you are in a constant time bind: you have no energy or time to look for and think about the real payoffs of your job. You become entrapped in an ocean of nonessential activities, losing the opportunity to spend time on those activities that would allow you to make a real contribution to your valued goals.

---

54   Do you have any suggestions on how I can track what I have already delegated?

If many routine activities have been delegated, check occasionally to see if they still need to be done at all. Subordinates have a way of continuing to do things you have forgotten about, activities that may no longer be necessary. It's good practice once in a while to ask your staff to do a time study along with you, paying particualr attention to the routine and habitual. Often these activities can be trimmed or eliminated.

After a task has been delegated, check back a week or a month later to determine if the activity still needs to be one. Don't assume that when the delegated activity becomes a misuse of time that it will automatically be discarded or that your people will check with you to see if it should still be done.

One manager found it valuable to set dates to review the delegated activity to determine whether it should be continued and to handle any problems with it. This regular check-up saved time and energy that otherwise would have been devoted to the doing of a delegated task no longer needed.

---

55   I have two subordinates who continually dump their problems on my shoulders instead of handling them themselves. What can I do?

It is sometimes useful to think of these kinds of problems or responsibilities as "monkeys" that are passed from subordinate to manager. When one feels a monkey sitting on one's back, there is a temptation to pass it on to someone else. In this case your subordinates are attempting illegitimately to pass monkeys on to you. What can you do?

Identify the problem as carefully as possible   Be as specific as you can about the condition of the "monkey": is there part of the problem that you are responsible for helping with?

Acknowledge that you are an unconscious fool for allowing your subordinates to dump on you You can generate 1001 excuses about why you permit it, but that's all they would be— excuses for not requiring your subordinates to be responsible for their jobs and excuses for their not allowing you to be responsible for yours.

Get clear about the purpose of your job Determine how these subordinate monkeys are affecting your job responsibilities, priorities, time, and energy. Unless you are being paid to take care of your subordinates' monkeys, which is highly unlikely, you are in a sense stealing from the company. That is, you are spending time at the subordinate level while receiving a manager's pay. Worse, you are not doing what you are truly being paid for because you are too busy caring for and feeding your subordinates' monkeys.

Get clear with the monkey passers that you will not accept their responsibilities anymore Renegotiate some of the implied or invisible agreements you have with your subordinates about monkey passing. You may want to prepare a statement to help get the problem in the proper perspective. For example: "Jim, I want you to know that I am here as your supervisor to help you with your problems (emphasize *your* because it is the subordinate's problem, first and foremost). I will continue to help you with your problem so long as we have an understanding that this problem is yours and not mine, and that you are being paid to manage it."

Establish a time and place for supporting your subordinates in handling their problems and monitoring their progress. Look closely at what it means when subordinates regularly get you to do their work and solve their problems. Some possible implications are:

- You have difficulty saying no to unreasonable requests because you want to feel needed, want to be accepted, or are unsure of your own management position.
- You have a set of invisible agreements that say in effect, "It is okay to dump into my Wheelbarrow of Time. I will handle it for you—I always have and I always will."
- You really don't know what your own job is as a manager, so you end up doing others' jobs for them.
- You would rather do their work than your own and possibly are misplaced in a management position.

---

56   How can I get my supervisor to delegate more responsibility to me?

Delegation can be a difficult management process, particularly if it is seen as "giving up part of my job" instead of as allowing the delegator more time to do his or her real job. Certainly you cannot force your supervisor to delegate more responsibility to you, but you can take thoughtful, purposeful action appropriate to your circumstances.

Make it easy for your manager to understand your professional interests and commitment, your abilities, and your career objectives Demonstrate that delegating work to you will benefit both of you as well as your organization. If you have a strong accounting and financial background or selling and marketing skills, outline ways that your talents can contribute to getting the job done now and in the future. If your manager doesn't know that you are good at graphics, by all means mention it.

Your organizational, financial, artistic, or editing abilities may be valuable assets that have been overlooked. Do not assume that your manager knows that you have these abilities—take responsibility to make sure that your skills are known. Do it in ways that make it easy to see the advantage of using your skills and abilities.

Take the initiative and do something that is significant but nonthreatening for your manager Take on an activity that you are not currently doing and that is not part of your overall job responsibilities. This might entail doing research on a project and presenting the data, completing a report that your manager usually does, or doing some accounting calculations that he or she normally would have to do.

Observe what others in positions similar to yours have done or are now doing that is valuable to their supervisors and organizations Often it is easier for your manager to accept your suggestions if you can show where a specific responsibility has been delegated effectively in other situations.

---

57   I am not always sure how much authority has been delegated to me. Is there a way to categorize the different levels of delegated authority?

There are of course degrees of delegation, and limits placed on authority. One way to understand what you can and cannot do is to divide your delegated authority into five broad categories or levels.

Level 1 *Act on your own—only routine reporting necessary*
At this level of authority you can simply act on your own when
appropriate (once a month, once a quarter, once a year),
keeping your manager informed of how you are doing. These
activities, from your manager's viewpoint, are those you can
carry out almost if not entirely on your own.

Level 2 *Act, but keep you manager advised of your actions*
As in level 1, you can act on your own, but here you must keep
your manager advised of your actions on some regular basis.
At this level, for whatever reasons, your manager is just a little
more concerned about your delegated authority; perhaps he or
she is not as sure about your competence or experience.
Whatever the reason, your manager needs to be kept more
closely informed of your activities on an ongoing basis.

Level 3 *Recommend—then take the agreed-to action*   At
this level, you do not have the delegated authority that you
have at level 1 and level 2. This could be for a number of
reasons. Your manager may have less control over this area
and may have to check out how your action will affect others in
the organization. Or your boss may be more sensitive or
cautious in this area, particularly if your actions impact more
fully on his or her own job responsibilities. In any event, for
you to take action without obtaining mutual agreement about
what you should do would be dangerous to your job future.

Level 4 *Ask—then take action only after your manager has
directed you to do so*   At this level, you have no delegated
authority to act or even to recommend a course of action. First,
ask your manager what should be done. While you may feel
that you have a right to take action or make a recommendation
in this area, your boss may not agree: to act or recommend
could offend your boss and jeopardize your career. This may
be unjust. Your boss may be underestimating your competence
and commitment and may not totally understand your

capabilities. But until they are understood, it is best to ask what is to be done. There is nothing worse than working for a nervous, angry boss, particulary if you are the one who caused the nervousness and anger.

Level 5 *Wait—act only after initiative has been taken by your manager* At this level of task performance, action on your part would almost certainly get you fired. In this area, your manager has not delegated any authority to you at all, not even authority to recommend or to ask; your actions, suggestions, and questions are plainly not wanted. For whatever reasons, justified or not, your boss is supersensitive in this area, so appropriate action is to do absolutely nothing.

All of these degrees of delegation and levels of authority may not exist in your relationship with your manager; it is possible that you and your manager have only levels 1, 2, and 3 and no levels 4 or 5. But don't assume that to be true without first checking and observing the realities of your relationship.

These five levels of delegation often apply to personal relationships. In your relationship with your spouse, for example, there are probably decisions you can make alone without any problem; but there may be other areas where your spouse would like to make a recommendation before a decision is made. Or there may be times when your spouse, rightly or wrongly, does not want your infinite wisdom and wise recommendations; your question is all that is acceptable. Further, there may be things about which your spouse does not even want you to ask.

Working Together: The Time-Conscious Management Team

There are only two forces that unite men—fear and interest.

Napoleon

Clapping with the right hand only will not produce a noise.

Malay Proverb

Taking charge of your time and work is not accomplished in a vacuum. It is often a partnership with others—a partnership that carries with it an entire set of agreements, understandings, and implied assumptions.

This chapter focuses on ways that successful, time-conscious management teams have found to work together. It expands the concept of team effort to include the idea that each of us is responsible for clarifying the agreements of our relationships, for letting others know what we expect from our own time and our time with them. It also deals with how to gain and retain respect from others for your time and how to balance the need to work with others' time demands and still meet your own.

---

58 How can I get others to respect my time more than they do now?

Gaining others' respect for your time is your own responsibility, and two things are required: first, you must respect your own time and make your words and actions demonstrate that respect; and second, you must respect the time of others, and demonstrate to them that you value their time.

One reality of time is that it is never totally your own. You must share it with others with whom you work, live, and interact. How that time is shared is negotiable, but the negotiation must be based on mutual respect for the value of time.

What follows is a list of ways in which you can gain respect for your time. Most of them, you will note, are also based on your respect for the time of others.

Be aware of how you use and misuse time   Get a firm grip on where your time goes. Become more conscious of time and ways you can more judiciously use it.

Be time discriminating   Base choices about how you use your time on your personal values and those of significant others. When you consistently use time in high-payoff ways, others can better understand what your priorities are and how their time contributes to getting those priorities done.

Communicate to others how you feel about their use of your time   If you think they are wasting your time—consciously or unconsciously—tell them so. Communicate your feelings in a thoughtful, appropriate way so they know how you feel and what you would like them to do.

Check out your invisible agreements   Many invisible agreements set up conditions that invite others to dump into your Wheelbarrow of Time. When you find that people are not respecting your time, look for the invisible agreements you have with them that allows that to happen. For example, if a co-worker continually keeps you waiting when you have an appointment, you probably have an invisible agreement that it's all right to be late, that you don't mind waiting—in short, that it's okay to waste your time.

Check out what statements are being made both verbally and, more significantly, nonverbally   Are others telling you (perhaps by their behavior) that:

- They don't respect your time because they feel you don't respect your own? Or theirs? Or both?
- They don't know they are disrespectful of your time?
- They don't agree that they *are* wasting your time?
- They aren't sure about your priorities, and what theirs should subsequently be?

Respect others' time   Demonstrate that you care about their time. Ask what you may be doing that wastes their time. Ask how you support them in managing their time, and what you could do to be more supportive. Don't underestimate the value of respecting others' time in encouraging them to respect your time more completely.

---

59   How can I demonstrate to my subordinates that I respect their time?

Observe how you interact with your subordinates   When you give work assignments are you clear about what you want done, how much authority you delegate, and what accountability you expect? Observe your management style. Make a selective time study and note your interactions with your subordinates. How many times during the day or week do you interrupt them? Were the interruptions legitimate? How many times were your personnel delayed in getting on with their work because you didn't get to them what they needed? Look at what you do that blocks their best performance.

Ask your subordinates, "What am I doing or not doing that wastes your time and acts as a barrier to getting your job done?" Don't ask them unless you want to hear the answer, because they just might tell you how much time you waste for them. This is good information to have, however, if you really want to hear.

Don't permit others to arbitrarily interrupt your meetings and conversations with your subordinates Show your respect for your subordinates and their time by notifying your secretary that you do not wish to be disturbed for the duration of the appointment. To be given second place to a telephone, for example, is particularly annoying. While we would clearly not allow someone to burst in on a meeting to ask an irrelevant question, it is amazing how often we will allow the telephone to interrupt.

Don't constantly interrupt your people with tasks for them to work on If you chart your daily interactions and the time spent with your subordinates, a multitude of unnecessary interruptions may show up. At minimum, check out your patterns of interrupting others consciously. How many of the interruptions that you make are unnecessary? Some interruptions probably could be batched together and brought to your subordinates' attention in a staff meeting or at some other convenient time.

Protect your subordinates' time Be conscious not only of how you may be infringing unproductively on your people's time but also of how others fail to respect their time, and of what you can do about it. Often you, their manager, are the culprit rather than others. For instance, be careful about volunteering your subordinates' time and services as if they were your own—a sure way to build resentment. And try to be there when your people need you. As one individual put it, "I am frustrated, no, I am damn resentful of the way my boss seems to disappear when I have conflicting demands made on me by his boss and other top management personnel. I don't feel it is my responsibility to choose between conflicting priorities of top management as they vie for my time. I feel my boss should show more respect for my time and run interference for me in these situations."

Take time to sit down with your people and discuss time-management philosophy and practices Acknowledge the importance of time—theirs and yours. Together search for ways that you can make more profitable use of your time, individually and as a team. The simple process of discussing effective time management demonstrates concern and respect for each other's time. One reality of time is that it is never totally your own. You must share it, as a manager, with others—with your boss, your subordinates, friends, and co-workers. How time gets shared, how much of it you give to your subordinates and how much of their time is available to you, is negotiable, but effective negotiating must be based on mutual respect for the value of time. It is a two-way street to be traveled by all members of the team: not just by your subordinates in their relationship to you, but also by you in your relationship with them.

Periodically take time to honestly express to your personnel how much you appreciate them and the way they support you. Let them know both in deed and word that you acknowledge the value of their time, that you are there to support them in every way to make the best use of their time. This respect and support will manifest itself in increased personal rapport with your people, increased productivity, and a sense of well-being and team effort for all.

---

60 I know that my agreements greatly affect my ability to manage my time. How can I be more conscious of them?

Agreements, both visible and invisible, conscious and unconscious, play a central role in managing your life and your time. But it is often the invisible agreements (understandings or unspoken expectations that you have with yourself or someone else) that do the most damage, because they go unnoticed and are more subtle.

For every time waster/pressure you have as a manager, as a parent, or as a friend, there almost certainly is an invisible agreement that says, in effect, that it is okay. In the case of a talkative co-worker, the invisible agreement between you and the friend is, "It is okay for you to come into my office and chitchat and rob me of my time. I will allow it and put up with it."

Other invisible agreements say, "I will allow you to waste my time; it is okay for you to continually impose on my time by asking me to do extra work. It is okay not to understand the assignments I have given you, because I will go over them again and again with you." You can also have invisible agreements with your family: "I will pick up after you, kids, it's okay," or, "I will act as your cab driver to school, club meetings, sports events, even when you could walk, take the bus, ride your bicycle, or make other arrangements."

Here are some checks and recommendations for dealing with agreements.

1 Continually be aware that the agreements you have, visible or invisible, have tremendous impact on your time and the quality of your daily living. These agreements can be unilateral, bilateral, or multilateral, and they affect not only your own effectiveness and well-being but also that of your significant others.

2 Evaluate on a regular basis your agreements with yourself and others in terms of that impact.

3 Look for the invisible agreement in each of your time wasters. Why are you saying, "It's okay for you to waste my time," or, "I am just a pushover for any of your dumb requests"?

4 Acknowledge your agreements with others and let them know, when approrpriate, how you feel about these agreements.

5 Be clear about your agreements and check to see if there is mutual understanding about what constitutes those agreements.

6 Move to renegotiate those agreements that no longer are working for you, that don't support your self-worth and sense of well-being.

Make agreements that support your work and life and monitor the quality of those agreements. Don't get stuck in agreements that worked for you last year but are no longer supportive of your goals. Honor your agreements, take responsibility for renegotiating the ones that are not working, and move to eliminate or create others as necessary.

---

61   How do I balance the desire to be available and the problem of subordinates just dropping in to chat?

This is a very common problem for busy executives. Here is what works for some:

Set aside a special time when your office door is open for anything your staff wishes to discuss   One manager made open-door time on Tuesday mornings between 9:00 and 11:00 and Thursday afternoons between 2:00 and 4:00.

Encourage (or require) all who come through your open door to think through what they want to talk to you about beforehand   You might say something like, "Please outline briefly what you would like to discuss with me so that I can do some preparation before we get together." This encourages staff members to do some prior thinking and gives you a chance to focus on the subject.

As part of your open-door policy, you may want to establish time limits, indicating the amount of time you have for a particular discussion   Say, "Lloyd, I have fifteen minutes. Is that going to be enough time for us to cover what you would like to discuss?"

Occasionally go to your subordinate's office to have a talk   It is easier to break off the conversation there and also gives you a chance to see what is happening down the line.

Define what an open-door policy means to you and to your subordinates, and imagine what it might contain It might look something like this.

- Respect and concern for time is expected during open-door minutes. Meetings are not a license to waste time.
- Management will be available as much as possible within the constraints of time and work responsibilities.
- Employees should think through what they expect from an open-door meeting. That doesn't mean that all meetings must result in earth-shaking decisions or even that the focus must always be exclusively on company business. It can be a "social" time, as long as it's used to mutual advantage.
- Management will help the staff with its problems, but the problems will still belong to staff members. Management does not expect to be saddled with them.
- The open-door policy is always open for review and change, in accord with what best supports the management team in effectively getting the job done.

---

62 How do I minimize excessive chitchat and conversation?

An unbelievable amount of time can be wasted on non-productive office chitchat—and excessive and peripheral conversation that does not support getting your job done. The culprits run the gamut from bosses to casual drop-in visitors.

Some small talk is normal and appropriate to most jobs, but conversational fat—nonproductive, excessive, mindless verbiage—is not. Strictly speaking, whenever a question can be answered with a simple yes or no or a brief explanation, anything added is fat. Detailed accounts, long-winded explanations, endless examples, rambling stories, tangential monologues, unnecessary definitions, and just plain, garden-variety gossip are all examples of conversational overkill.

Strive for a happy medium: a balance between saying what is essential and what is socially required. You can attempt to find that balance by considering the following suggestions and questions:

1 Listen to what is being said, by yourself and others. How much is pertinent to the purpose of the conversation?

2 Track everything that is irrelevant. Who started it? Who contributed to it? Who cut it off and pulled the conversation back to the main track?

3 How much time do you spend on small talk?

4 What would happen to your office relationships or intra-office communication if conversational fat were eliminated?

5 If you had only three minutes to get the message across, what would you cut out of your ten-minute talk?

6 If each word cost you a dollar, would you make your three-minute talk even shorter?

7 If each word in excess of 250 cost $10, how would you say it?

Excessive talk has killed many a sale and more than one friendship. Work to short-circuit it by getting to the point quickly and staying on track. Work on your own attitude. If you tend to be purposeful and are clear, direct, and conscious of other people's time, then others will respect your time.

Some friendly social conversation is needed and desirable for establishing and maintaining mutually satisfying and meaningful relationships. It is the excessive—the mindless, irrelevant rambling on and on—that is to be guarded against. The correct balance in your conversation between appropriate social dialogue and conversational fat is a matter of judgment.

---

63   How do I make my manager understand what my job duties and responsibilities are?

There is a myth in management today that the boss understands everything that subordinates should be doing or actually are doing. It is probable, however, that your manager does not completely understand your job duties or the extent of your responsibilities. And ironically, the better you perform your duties, the less aware your manager will be of specifically what you do.

One thing is almost certain: your manager is unaware of how much time it takes you to accomplish most tasks, and he or she does not give serious thought to how additional work will affect your time or your ability to complete the job. This may be wrong, unfair, or even bad management, but it is often a reality to be dealt with.

The following points may help in correcting this situation.

Take 100 percent responsibility for realizing that your manager does not understand what your job duties entail or how much time they take   The problem is not your boss's as much as it is yours.

Think through some ways to solve the problem If appropriate, tell your manager how you feel about the situation and what your solutions are.

Rewrite your job description Drop activities you feel should not be part of your job and add activities that ought to be included. Go over this job description with your manager to help him or her understand what jobs are particularly time-consuming. The more accurately you can determine how much time each activity takes, the better for both you and your boss.

Make a time study for a few days Log your duties and the time spent on them. This time log can be invaluable to you in measuring the specific ways your time is mortgaged and the demands that are made on it. It is much more graphic than simply talking about how much time you spend sitting in meetings, working with your staff, or corresponding with the head office to justify this or that management action. A time log provides you with an accurate, objective picture.

Show your manager what you are working on when you are actually doing it This gives a firsthand impression of what you're talking about and enables your boss to interact with you—to make suggestions for eliminating, deferring, reducing, or delegating certain tasks.

Do a task analysis Identify the purpose of each task and how you do it—what you could eliminate, what someone else could do, what you could do in less time or less carefully, what activities you could batch together, and what activities lend themselves to regrouping. Take the initiative and propose better ways of doing your work, thinking through time-saving approaches and discussing them with your supervisor.

Brainstorm with your supervisor ways to save time The free flow of ideas often stimulates new thinking and helps you to develop new methods for accomplishing more in less time. Concerted steps can then be taken to relieve job pressure. At minimum, your manager will become more sensitive to your job responsibilities and the ways your time is used, an understanding that will help both of you to be more objective and realistic.

Suggest that your supervisor switch jobs with you for one day Be judicious—not every manager is open to such a suggestion. If your manager does your job for a day, he or she will understand as never before how you spend your time and why your work takes the time it does. You will benefit just as much by handling your manager's work for a day.

---

64   I am not clear about my professional roles and responsibilities, and I am uneasy about what is expected of me.

Unclear roles and responsibilities can cause enormous losses of time and effectiveness for all concerned. The clearer the agreements, expectations, roles, and responsibilities, the better chance one has of managing his or her time well. The following three statements illustrate typical related problems.

- I have been assigned two titles or areas of responsibility recently in our organization. My time is divided, and how much time I should be devoting to each has never been defined. I feel that I am doing a half-job in both areas. I would like to get that cleared up.

A time study would help determine how much and where time is spent in both these areas, as well as indicating what tasks need more time given them. In addition, some tasks need to be analyzed to help determine how much time should be spent. At minimum, a time and task analysis charting could act as a point of reference for subordinate and manager to begin to clarify how much time should be spent in each area. It is possible that the boss doesn't have the answer either and would profit from seeing the data you collect.

- I would like to make it clear to other department managers that I have the ability and permission to assign work to their people on a project basis.

From where does this permission or authority come? Do other department managers fully understand your role relative to them? You may be seen as a threat, going around them and subverting their authority in the eyes of their people. A department managers' meeting to clarify feelings and expectations is often helpful. Respective bosses may need to get together to clarify this problem if you cannot resolve the situation.

- I would like to know more clearly what my new management job is and what is expected of me. Everybody in the office seems to have their own thoughts about what my job is and what it is not.

If it is a new management position, a first step is to work closely with your immediate manager to determine what the roles and expectations are. If you are in doubt about whether you are responsible for a particular area, check it out. In addition to your boss, run your observations and considerations by someone who can help, such as a co-worker. You may be in a trial and error position where your job has a lot of flexibility and is, in part, open-ended. Many jobs are what you are willing and able to make them. This can be seen by you either as an opportunity for growth or as a real threat to your security, depending on how you choose to perceive it.

Whatever the particular role and responsibility is that you may want to clear up, it is up to you. That is, you are 100 percent responsible for getting as clear as you can about what it is that is expected of you in your position. You have the right and the responsibility to ask as many questions as you need to ask to get clear about your job duties. Don't wait for your boss to volunteer this information. Take the responsibility and find out what you need to know to do the job that you are being paid to do.

---

65   How do I say no to inappropriate demands on my time and make it clear that I really mean it?

One of the most important and responsible ways to improve your effectiveness is to learn the art of saying no to requests on your time. In fact, it is impossible to manage your time effectively until you establish the parameters of your goodwill and establish what you are willing and able to say no to.

Saying no protects your time from unwanted demands and conserves precious time that is then available for higher-priority tasks. You certainly don't do your manager, your friend, or your spouse any great favors when you say yes to a request that you would have said no to if you had been responsibly managing your time.

Your ability (or more correctly, your responsibility) to say yes or no to time demands depends upon the various roles you have chosen to play and the agreements you have made, invisible and visible. We all play different roles in life— employee, citizen, friend, spouse, parent, church member— and their accompanying agreements impact on our ability to say no. If you have no agreements to the contrary and your role does not obligate you to say yes to a request on your time, then you are a free agent and can simply say no.

Once you have established your right to refuse demands on your time, these techniques can support your decision to say no and mean it.

Clarify how you want to spend your time   The clearer you are about what you want to say yes to, the easier it is to say no to a request that doesn't fit into that picture. Then you can honestly say, "No, I am sorry, I have a prior time commitment." And you do have another commitment—to a valued goal with higher priority.

Acknowledge that there is never enough time in life   When you say no, you are not necessarily denying the worth or importance of the request; you are simply acknowledging a time reality—that there is not time to do everything.

Be sure that you know what the request really is   Ask for further clarification. This shows that you are listening and may allow you to suggest how the request can be fulfilled in other ways, even though you yourself are saying no.

If you want to say no now but leave the door open to saying yes later, do it   "No, I am sorry, I have a prior time commitment now. But, if you want, why don't you check back with me in a few days (weeks, months)?"

You might want to give a qualified no   You might say, "I am sorry that I must say no to your request, but if you will do the following, I will be able to help you." Spell out what the other person must do—undertake further research, get others' help lined up before you commit yourself, do part of the job first before asking you for your time, or whatever.

A useful technique in saying no to a request on your time is scripting: that is, developing a preplanned response to specific situations that produce demands on your time. Scripting is especially helpful in handling predictable difficulties, such as getting stuck on the phone with a talkative but important client or having inordinate demands on your time made by your boss. The scripts should (1) be prepared before the confrontation, (2) express your attitudes accurately, including your positive and negative feelings, (3) be practical, and (4) be tailored to the particular situation you want to handle.

Possible scripts might look like these:

Jim, I am sorry, but I can't help you this week on the advertising proposal. Have you checked with Susan to see if she can assist you?

or

John, I appreciate your asking me to attend the two-day conference, but I'm sorry, I have a prior time commitment.

A word of caution. You have in a sense forfeited your right to say no to a request on your time if in fact you have already agreed to say yes through some kind of invisible agreement or as part of a role you are playing. In that case, you have, in effect, a bilateral or multilateral agreement, and if you move to break it unilaterally you can cause serious trouble for yourself. Move first to clarify real expectations and then move to renegotiate your agreement with the person to whom you want to say no.

If you cannot successfully renegotiate the agreement, you may still opt to say no and live with the consequences. But in almost every case, it is a better course to gain the agreement of others concerning what they can legitimately expect from you and you from them.

You are 100 percent responsible for establishing the parameters of your goodwill to others. You are responsible for controlling your work and life, the quality of your agreements, and the kinds of games and roles you choose to play.

---

66   Why do I make time commitments to my boss and others that I know I can't keep?

There may be many reasons for an inordinate need to say yes to unreasonable assignments—the wish to be seen as a "good" person, the desire to please, a low self-image, or a feeling that others will not like you or respect you if you say no.

One thing needs to be understood at the start: you do your manager and associates no favor by committing yourself to do something that you can't do. It is far better to be honest with them from the beginning and say that you would like to do this for them, but that you don't see a way to find time. You may have an unconscious agreement that it is okay for others to make time demands on you even when it is clear that you can't get them done. But agreeing to do something when you know you won't do it is a losing proposition for all concerned.

Evaluate your need to please and your need to say yes to impossible or unwanted requests on your time Check out what needs are fulfilled by your actions. What are the payoffs for you and others, both negative and positive, for saying yes when you wanted to say no? What do you get to think, feel, or do because of your saying yes? Do you get to think you are superhuman, the doer of impossible tasks, or do you get to feel victimized by these unfair time demands? Do you get to avoid what you should really be doing?

Identify specific areas for which you are failing to take responsibility when you commit yourself to doing what you won't have time to do If you say yes to these requests, will you fail to find time for important planning, for reevaluating certain office procedures, or for thinking of better ways of accomplishing your goals?

Clarify the problem. Try to be clear about when it happens, what it pertains to, and to whom you commit your time. For example, is your time overcommitted to projects that you like to do or projects you don't like to do? Are they projects you can do easily or projects you find difficult (if not impossible) to do, even when you have the time? Under what circumstances do you make these commitments—when the people requesting them are angry? nice? pleading? when they are under pressure? when you owe them a favor?

Identify the situation's agreements, both visible and invisible What needs to be renegotiated? What needs to be eliminated? Is there an agreement implied between you and the requester that you will always say yes and attempt to commit time even when it is impossible? You may want to change this. Perhaps you need to establish an agreement that time requirements will be mutually explored before you commit yourself to certain projects and that your commitment will be contingent on whether that time is available.

Prepare a ready response to the expected request of your time   Preplanned responses should accurately express your attitude (including your positive and negative feelings), be practical, and be tailored to the particular situation you want to confront and manage.

An example of a script might be "George, I want to get that report out for you and I know you want it. But it would be unfair to both of us if I agreed to do it when I know that I do not have the seven hours today or tomorrow to do it. Do you have any suggestions on how we might accomplish this?"

---

67   A lot of time is wasted redoing tasks that should have been done right the first time. My subordinates don't seem to know what their assignments are.

It is definitely a handicap for you to be well organized and clear about what you have to do while your subordinates are ineffectually managing their time. But time management encompasses the efficient use of your own time as well as the management of others and their time, and managers can help their subordinates operate more effectively. Listed below are guidelines for making task assignments to staff personnel.

Make an effort to estimate how much time an assignment will take, even if it is only a rough calculation   If you have an idea how much time is needed, then it will be easier to understand when and where to invest this time.

Many subordinates fail to complete assignments simply because there is never enough time to do them in the first place.

Ask your personnel what they think is a realistic time estimate for an assignment. It is frequently better to leave some tasks unattended than to attempt to give them less time than necessary. Inefficiency, misunderstandings, or sloppy results often accompany unrealistic time estimates.

Explain the task clearly   Ask your personnel to repeat back to you in their own words what they understand their assignments to be. The additional time necessary is time well spent and at the same time allows you both to explore more productive avenues for accomplishing the task.

Explain how a task fits into the total scheme of things and how it supports the valued goals of the team, the department, and the organization. Understanding the why of an assignment can help personnel to understand how it should be done.

Review task assignments together in the context of valued goals, priorities, and proper time investments   You both may discover too much time is being spent on some tasks while not enough is being invested on others. Knowing the valued goals of the management team and organization clarifies the what and the why of task assignments. Many subordinates in part don't know what their tasks are because they don't know what the goals are and don't understand their specific contribution to the whole.

Take the time to discover what your personnel think are realistic work assignments   Seek to understand what influences them in their efforts to get the job done. What are the circumstances that impact on task accomplishment? Do they face certain constant stops and starts, interruptions, or distractions? Are there times during the day that are slow and others that are hectic? What impinges on their concentration and effectiveness?

Many subordinates have expressed the wish that their managers would take the time to find out what is really happening on the "firing line." As one frustrated subordinate put it, "Tasks are given to me but I have little or no real idea of how it all fits together. When I ask my manager how this assignment fits our purpose, I usually get a vague and often mumbled answer that doesn't enlighten me in any way."

Take the time to learn as much as possible about your people's workloads Concern yourself particularly with the little details that take their time and sap their energy. Then they will know that you understand what they are facing, and you will be in a better position to know what they can handle.

The frustration that some subordinates feel is expressed in the following statement: "I would like my boss to handle my job for one day. I think she would have an entirely different picture of what I do and would understand why certain things take so much time to complete. It would make her a better boss, I am sure."

Ask your subordinates to outline their job duties and responsibilities as they see them Have them indicate how they think you, their manager, see their duties and responsibilities—what agreements govern them, how important their tasks are, what your expectations are, and how well you think they are doing.

Similarly, you analyze their job duties as you see them and compare your list with your subordinate's. Probably substantial differences will surface—different expectations, different definitions of job responsibilities, and different evaluations of how the tasks are being performed. This valuable information will help not only in discussing current assignments but also will lay a foundation for future ones.

Don't leave work assignments until the last minute This causes unnecessary rush jobs and time pressures for your personnel. Don't impose unrealistic time demands on a task, particularly when your own failure to plan and perform caused the delay in the first place.

Don't assume that your subordinates have nothing to do
They are not simply waiting for you to give them work so they will have something to do. Understand what their work flow requirements are.

If your subordinates don't know what you want them to do, whose problem is that and who is the principal cause of that problem? Reflect on your past and current relationship with your own manager. What did you like best about the manner in which your manager assigned tasks to you? What did you like least? Observe managers and how they delegate and follow through on tasks. What works and what doesn't work? Assuming your subordinates want to understand what to do, it is up to both you and them as a team to enhance the understanding needed to get the job done right the first time.

---

68   How can I get by without a secretary?

A good secretary no doubt can help you be more effective, but what happens when you don't have a secretary? How can you survive? Here are some practical strategies.

Make good use of others' staff support   A client's secretary, for example, often can obtain material you need for a meeting with her boss or give reminders of commitments made to you. Staff members often are willing to do something extra for you if you appreciate their effort and if it helps their managers.

Learn from others' secretaries how they organize and plan not only their own work but the work of their managers   You can learn how to set up your own tickler file system or how to record phone calls, using methods that take little time while greatly increasing office efficiency.

Make use of temporary help to get out a backlog of correspondence or handle an overload of routine but necessary clerical work   An occasional investment in temporary help can free you for the more important tasks that you and only you can perform.

Make use of time-saving services.

- Telephone answering services or recorders.
- Mailgrams.
- Speedy-reply forms.
- Express mail services.

---

69   At times my boss is my biggest time waster. How do I handle this and prevent it from happening?

It is common to hear from managers and professionals that their bosses waste their time by being indecisive, getting off track, being disorganized, assigning tasks that are either unnecessary or of minimal importance, failing to set definite and realistic goals, and not respecting subordinates' time.

But it is important to understand that, even though you feel certain that your boss is wasting your time, your boss may not necessarily agree. In fact, you can pretty much assume your manager does not consider your assignments or his or her management style as time wasting. This does not negate nor diminish your experience that your boss sometimes wastes your time—it simply puts it in a more realistic perspective.

It is also important to remember that your manager is your principal source of imposed time and that the requests made by your boss are of significant and unique importance. In addition, your career path in your organization lies with your boss and, while it is possible to move to another position within the company if you don't get along well, it may be difficult.

These reminders are only meant to emphasize the importance and the challenge you have in managing not only your own time but the time pressures imposed on you by this important person in your work life—your boss.

Yet, it is only natural at times to feel that your boss is imposing on you inappropriately, doesn't understand the time pressures you face, or is inconsiderate of your job responsibilities. There are many ways of approaching these problems.

1 Note again that it is *your* opinion that your boss is wasting your time—not your boss's. Even if he or she assigns you an activity to work on immediately when you are up to your ears in other priorities, your boss is not seeing it as a time waster.

2 Be specific about what you consider to be a time waster. Is it the timing of assignments? Perhaps your boss has given you something to do that will take two days; yet he or she wants it done immediately. Or is it a time waster in your

view because it is already being done by someone else, or because it occurs too frequently? By being as clear as possible you can separate what you feel are legitimate calls upon your time from what you feel to be illegitimate ones.

3   Check to determine what you may have done to cause this time waster from your boss. Have you been clear about what your priorities are? Have you kept your boss informed on where you are on required projects? Maybe your boss doesn't know that your time is already over-committed. Perhaps he or she expects you to say if and when an assignment is unreasonable from your point of view. Do you expect your boss to know just how busy you are and how you feel about handling another report, attending a meeting, or interrupting your work to attend to a minor request?

4   Relieve your boss of having to be a mind reader. Do you require your boss to read your mind and be supersensitive to your feelings? When you receive a questionable assignment or when you are interrupted, let your boss know that you feel he or she is inappropriately imposing on your time. Most bosses would flunk Mind Reading 101. Their clairvoyance is limited.

One junior manager continually complained about his boss, who imposed one priority after another on him, shifted priorities, and constantly interrupted him throughout the day to check on how he was coming along. These constant interruptions and changing priorities were driving him crazy and wasting a lot of his time. Yet, never once had he taken 100 percent responsibility for this experience by acknowledging his feelings and then appropriately communicating them to his boss. When his boss realized how this subordinate felt, he immediately met with him to identify the problems and discuss how they might work them out.

5 Make a time study and log how you are spending your time, paying particular attention to the problem area. Most bosses have no idea how much time anything that they assign to you takes. Making a time study to show where your time actually goes can help clarify how your time is being used.

6 Make a list of how much time each task takes, noting which items that have been given you by your boss and whether you feel they are taking too much of your time. It is far easier for your boss to see what you are talking about if you present a specific list of how much time an assignment will take or how much time it takes to stop what you are doing and discuss another project. You can also spell out what is not going to get done if you are taken off one assignment and given another. This list can provide your boss with an avenue for readjusting priorities and time commitments and for realigning job assignments if necessary.

When confronting inappropriate demands on your time, be careful not to overreact to these requests and end up wasting more time than the time waster itself did. It is easy to gripe and moan about how bad it is to have a disorganized or inconsiderate boss and end up wasting even more time in complaining, feeling sorry for ourselves, and being resentful.

Your relationship with your boss is your prime time relationship—one that can interrupt your day faster, change your priorities around quicker, and kick your "things to do" list into a cocked hat faster than any other. You have a major responsibility to your boss and he or she to you. You do no great favors if you feel your boss is a big time waster and don't do something about it.

70   How can I support my boss's time more fully and, at the same time, get support for my time?

Every management team is different and there is no single blueprint for achieving an effective, time-conscious management team. Here is a selective checklist that provides a practical guide to develping a time-conscious team effort. Review it with a critical eye, open to what might work for you. Which suggestions would enhance the effectiveness and time consciousness of your management team? Some of them are ones that you may already be practicing. Others will not seem important. Most are worth your testing and testing, again and again.

1   Do understand what your manager expects of you. Does your manager expect you to work overtime when there is extra work to be done? Does your manager expect you to level with him or her about how you feel about what is happening at work?

   One junior subordinate complained that he never knew what his manager expected of him, didn't know what his priorities should be. Yet, on discussing this, it was clear that this junior manager had never really asked for clarification of goals and objectives. He had never sat down with his boss to communicate his uncertainty about what the real expectations and agreements were regarding his role in the company.

2   Do clarify what are prime and secondary priorities with your boss. Check to see what your manager's priorities are and observe how your manager reacts to your priorities. Try to get an overall sense of what both of you see as

important. When you are not sure, ask. Priority clarification is essential to developing and maintaining an effective management-team relationship.

Many subordinate managers complain that they never know what their bosses want them to do, that priorities are unclear or shifting. Time spent clarifying and getting agreement on priorities with your boss is high-payoff time. The key to getting things done is placing high priorities on the right activities.

3   Do understand your job responsibilities and areas of accountability. Distinguish between those activities that are relatively low payoff but still have to be done and those activities that are high payoff and vital. Know when and where to take the initiative and when and where your boss doesn't want your opinion and certainly not your independent action. Understand what delegated responsibility and accountability mean to your boss, to you, and to your success in your organization.

4   Do realize that the more time you invest in understanding what your manager wants you to do and where your manager wants you to go, the less time you will waste getting back from where you shouldn't have been in the first place—and the less anxiety you will cause. It is rough working for a nervous manager, particularly when you are responsible for the nervousness. It may be entirely unfair or irrational for your manager to be upset with you, but it can happen nevertheless—and you certainly don't need an anxious boss on your hands. Understanding what your manager wants will help prevent this.

5   Do put yourself in your manager's position and attempt to see the world from your manager's point of view. Understanding and respecting your manager's needs and responsibilities will go a long way toward successful supporting of his or her time.

Here are some examples of what *not* to do, things that don't support the time-conscious management team.

1   Don't be confused about who is boss—your manager is. You boss's duties and responsibilities are different from yours and are distinctly his or hers. Your manager is responsible in areas that you are not.

2   Don't expect everything in your relationship with your boss to be fair. Life isn't fair, sometimes not even rational or reasonable. It isn't fair for your manager to ask you to take on additional assignments—especially assignments you feel are out of your work area—particularly when you are overworked as it is. It isn't fair that your boss expects your full support even when he or she doesn't seem to support you very well. Nevertheless, that may be the case.

3   Don't promise what you can't deliver. When you are asked to do something, and you know that you can't get it done when or in the way your boss wants and expects it, speak up. You were not hired as a miracle worker and you can't be expected to leap tall buildings or even short ones.

4   Don't make excuses for why you didn't get a particular job done or why you made a mistake. Your boss isn't paying for excuses, and excuses are a way of avoiding responsibility for what you are being paid to do. Excuses may get you off the hook temporarily, but they can easily become your reality and leave you believing all the reasons you made up for not completing the job. When you believe that you could have gotten the reports done on time if your secretary had been better organized or that you could have done a better job in planning if others had cooperated with you more, you are probably deceiving yourself.

5   Don't pull any fast ones on your boss. Keep your manager informed when he or she needs or wants to be informed. Work to minimize unpleasant surprises. When in doubt

about what you should keep your manager informed on, check it out.

6 Don't expect to change your manager. Your manager is who he or she is, and you must work with that. You cannot change anyone except yourself. Certainly, you can create an environment to support change—you can possibly make your boss thirst for change—but you can't do the changing.

7 Don't lay unrealistic expectations on your boss that can't be lived up to. He or she is only human. When you expect your manager always to be sensitive to your needs, to be thoughtful, polite, and kind all the time, and to be thinking of how you are feeling and what you want, you are setting you both up for real disappointment.

8 Don't carry a grudge against your boss, no matter how right you may be. You do yourself and your boss no favors by harboring resentment and working to even the score. The last thing your manager needs is someone who is resentful and set on getting even.

9 Don't be afraid to disagree with your boss, but do so in a way that will support the team effort and not make your manager wrong. Often the way that you offer your point of view is more important than the particular viewpoint you hold. When you communicate your thoughts in ways that are supportive (rather than concentrating strictly on your own needs and point of view), it is easier for your manager to see and accept them.